Twilight of British Rail?

Twilight of British Rail?

Michael R. Bonavia, MA, PhD, FCIT

DAVID & CHARLES

Newton Abbot   London   North Pomfret (Vt)

British Library Cataloguing in Publication Data

Bonavia, Michael R.
  Twilight of British Rail?
  1. British Rail
  I. Title
  385'.0941   HE3020.B76

  ISBN 0–7153–8625–5

Photoset by
Northern Phototypesetting Co. Bolton
and printed in Great Britain
by Butler and Tanner Ltd, Frome and London
for David & Charles (Publishers) Limited
Brunel House Newton Abbot Devon

Published in the United States of America
by David & Charles Inc
North Pomfret Vermont 05053 USA

Contents

A Personal Note

In my earlier books, *The Four Great Railways* which covered the period from grouping in 1923 to nationalisation in 1948, and *British Rail: the First 25 Years* which brought the narrative to 1973, I endeavoured to be as historically accurate and objective as I was able, keeping personal opinions and judgments to a minimum. The present work, although in some ways a sequel to those earlier studies, is frankly subjective, as an attempted picture 'warts and all', of BR in the mid-eighties. I hope it will not give offence to those who are still coping with problems that do not afflict a retired railwayman, even though they may well disagree with my observations and dismiss my suggestions.

It can reasonably be argued that, upon accepting a pension, one should keep one's mouth shut and leave one's still active colleagues to get on with the job, refraining from uninvited commentary. On the other hand, once involved in railway work it is difficult to disengage, to lose interest in what is happening and become a silent spectator. And occasionally, as the years go by, vivid parallels with past experiences seem to arise. Let that be my explanation if not my excuse.

M.R.B.

Haslemere, Surrey
December 1984

1

British Rail After 35 Years

The term 'twilight' in the title of this book should not be misunderstood. It is used in the old Anglo-Saxon sense of 'between-light', which can herald a dawn as well as a slide into darkness. My belief is that the 1980s may well decide which of these two experiences is going to befall BR, and it is high time that BR's proprietor – meaning the nation, as represented by the Government – finally decides what is to be done about this immensely valuable property which it owns.

For it *is* an immensely valuable property even if it is not returning cash profits to the national exchequer. Some people have cast greedy eyes upon its break-up value, wanting to sell off its 10,500 miles of reserved, well-engineered rights of way all over the country as well as many valuable urban sites. Others, scenting lucrative contracts for concreting over rail tracks, have been lobbying to obtain Government support for rail-road conversion schemes. Picking out tit-bits of profitable rail-associated businesses, and handing them over to private purchasers, has been a form of asset-stripping under the broad banner of privatisation.

Why is the railway business vulnerable to this sort of thing, and apparently short of influential friends? After all, despite a slight slip in standards insofar as passenger fatalities were concerned in 1984 including one accident caused by a cow, railways nevertheless clearly represent the safest form of inland transport. In 1982, for the fourth year out of the previous seven, not a single passenger was killed in a train accident; even in the 20 years from 1964 to 1983 only 198 passengers were killed in train accidents in Britain, and of those 113 resulted from four disasters. Compared with the thousands killed annually on the roads this is a remarkable record.

Rail is very often the quickest form of transport, especially over medium distances of which there are so many in Britain. It is usually also the most comfortable – one can read, eat and drink, converse or sleep far better than in cars or even planes. Lastly, it is much the least environmentally damaging system, as anyone living next to a motorway, under an airport flight path, or inhabiting what was formerly a quiet village now shaken day and night by juggernaut lorries, or a suburban street where these monsters park at night, can testify. It makes no demands on our precious remaining acres in the way that land-hungry motorways and airports do. Its air pollution, especially when electrified, is negligible compared with its competitors, and its visual intrusions into the landscape, mellowed by time, are usually items on the credit more than the debit side.

So why has this highly civilised form of transport declined to the extent described on page 11? This book is not a public relations exercise for BR, and in trying to analyse the reasons which have led to the relative decline of the railways, I have allowed myself to be critical of some past policies at railway headquarters. But one must avoid over-simplified conclusions. One is that *all* the trouble springs from under-investment by Governments, although this is undoubtedly an important factor. Another puts the blame on truculence and short-sightedness on the part of the trade unions, which again is a factor, but only a partial one.

One of the silliest criticisms levelled at railway managers has been that they indulge in 'playing trains' and lack the business approach which only an injection of talent from, say, Marks & Spencer can rectify. Performance in any activity is enhanced if there is dedication and enthusiasm over and above the need to earn a living. We do not criticise hospital staffs for 'playing doctors and nurses'. Pride in the job, some degree of personal commitment, is essential in any service industry. And railways are just that: partly a service and partly an industry. It is wishful thinking to try to push them into either category exclusively, though it might suit, in one direction, some Conservative politicians and, in the other, some trade union leaders. The art of successful railway management, as was the case even under private ownership, has always been to contrive the best blend of the two influences. Today's British Railways

Board is walking that tightrope as skilfully as it can – in the face of constant jerking from the ends!

Some of the views expressed in this book may seem heretical, as for example, a certain scepticism about the long-term benefits from the over-rigid application of cost accounting to policy decisions, which has dominated thinking for something like 30 years inside BR. In a business producing a range of goods for different markets, it makes sense to cost each product as closely as possible in relation to the actual or potential revenue obtainable from it. But transport is often saleable only as a total package; separate costing of each component, and discarding fragments that seem non-viable, may render the total package either unsaleable or much less saleable. For instance, too much penny-pinching in the provision of lavatories and other terminal facilities, and the selective withdrawal of catering facilities on trains, may do ultimate damage to the passenger business far exceeding the immediate cash saving.

But to start with it is useful in analysing how our railways came to be in what the Victorians liked to call 'reduced circumstances', to set the record straight in some respects. There are conflicting and often mistaken views about how British Rail today compares with the railways before nationalisation, or indeed before they were subject to Government control during the 1939–45 war. On the one hand there is perhaps overmuch nostalgia for the age of steam and too easy an assumption that rail travel used to be more enjoyable as well as more interesting an experience than it is today. It was not always so. On the other hand, there is the erroneous impression, held even by some people who should know better, that the private railway companies were bankrupt and that they had to be nationalised on that account.

The facts are that in 1939 (which is a better comparison than the last year before nationalisation, 1947, because of the distorting effect of the war years) railway services were patchy. Some were absolutely excellent, many adequate, and a few pretty poor. Equally, the railways were far from bankrupt; they earned working surpluses sufficient to pay interest on their debentures and (usually) also on their preference stocks, though what was left for the ordinary shareholders was only enough for small dividends at best. In consequence, new investment funds were impossible to obtain from the stock market; renewals and improvements had to be financed either from internal sources – from reserve funds, in fact – or by borrowing with some form of Government assistance at specially favourable interest rates.

During the second world war the railways were 'conned' (the word is used deliberately) by the Government in 1941 into accepting an agreement under which they received a fixed 'rental' for their undertakings which then operated under Government instructions, the State taking the receipts through the Control Agreement and meeting the expenditure from the same source. This meant that the railways obtained no benefit from carrying the swollen wartime traffics; in fact, the 'rental' payments available for the shareholders amounted to only 67 per cent of the actual net receipts the railways earned, pocketed by the Treasury, in 1941; under 48 per cent in 1942; 41 per cent in 1943; and 48 per cent in 1944. Over these four years they earned £350 millions net but received only £174 millions of this money back. Then in 1948 they were nationalised, the compensation being based on a Stock Exchange valuation of this depressed rental income. Sharp practice? Well, rather close to it.

An attempt to justify these imposed terms was made by the ebullient Dr Hugh Dalton (the then Chancellor of the Exchequer later sacked for an indiscreet pre-Budget remark) by describing the railways as a poor bag of assets. This was largely untrue and wholly unfair; the infrastructure was pretty well intact, but locomotives and rolling stock had been over-worked and under-maintained to meet Government requirements and regulations during the war. This had been recognised by the creation of an Arrears of Maintenance Trust Fund, into which the repairs and renewals provisions that had become overdue were paid. But did the railways benefit from this after nationalisation? Not at all. The fund (represented by holdings in Government stocks) was thrown into the pot of the British Transport Commission, which had many interests besides the nationalised railways, and was used for various non-railway purposes, including purchase of road haulage businesses which competed with the railways!

Forgetting these unhappy episodes, let us go back to the immediate pre-war period to compare railways 'then' with railways 'now'. At the end of the last pre-war year – ie December 1938 – the comparison of route-miles shows the present system as about 55 per cent of the pre-war figure. Passenger carriages are about 40 per cent of pre-war, but wagons are only an amazing 10 per cent of the earlier figure, and far less if the former total of private owners' wagons is brought into the comparison. These represented nearly as large a fleet as that of the railways in 1938; today, though such wagons in modern form are still a substantial proportion of total wagon stock, it is small in comparison with the pre-war fleet.

One cannot compare traction units in any meaningful way. Against some 19,600 steam locomotives in 1938 there are today only about 2,600 diesel locomotives and 250 electric locomotives; but so much traction is performed by multiple-units in which power is dispersed through the train in different forms and combinations that comparisons are really of little value, even if they can be made at all.

Much more important, however, is a comparison of today's work-load with that of the pre-war steam railways. Here is the shortest possible summary: more figures are in the Statistical Appendix.

	Millions	
	1938	*1983*
Passenger journeys	1,236	695
Freight tons handled	289*	145
Freight ton-miles	16,672*	10,653

So, passenger journeys are 56 per cent of pre-war. Passenger-miles would be a better comparison, but 1938 figures are not available. An informed guess, taking into account the increase in the average length of journey, would be that they are now between 85 and 90 per cent of pre-war. Freight is 50 per cent of pre-war in originating traffic, or 64 per cent on a tonne-mile

---

* Tons in published figures have been adjusted to tonnes for comparative purposes.

11

basis. If one looks at the vast reduction in the stock of both passenger carriages and (even more) wagons, it is clear that very much more intensive utilisation is being practised. Efficiency is greatly improved in that sense.

How is it that with a wagon fleet so tiny in comparison with that of 1938, between one-half and two-thirds of the freight work is being done? The reasons are varied. First, the work has changed in character, train-load business overwhelmingly replacing wagonload and thereby vastly improving utilisation in the form of tonne-miles per wagon per annum. Average length of haul has increased as the figures clearly show. Then, a fleet of privately-owned wagons (not of course comparable in numbers with that of pre-war days) has been built up in recent years and this does not appear in the BR statistics.* Lastly, average wagon capacity has greatly increased.

Staff productivity, also, has increased. The railways of today are doing about half the work of the pre-war steam railways with little more than a quarter of the pre-war staff. The 1983 total of 197,000 employees in the railways, workshops and rail catering can be *roughly* compared with more than half a million pre-war. (An exact comparison cannot be made because of the 'hiving-off' of various activities and other changes.)

But this is not a cause for complacency if the market is going to continue to shrink. Are the improvements in productivity sufficient by comparison with, for example, what is happening in other forms of transport, let alone manufacturing industry? And what is the quality of the product; can it hold or increase its share of the market?

Let us forget the war and immediate post-war years and the restrictions that they imposed and look at the last time when the railways were working as truly private-enterprise businesses, pursuing their own objectives. All four great companies had been managed by outstanding leaders, two of whom (Sir Herbert Walker and Sir Ralph Wedgwood) had just retired, though Lord Stamp and Sir James Milne were still in charge at Euston and Paddington respectively. Lord Stamp, a distinguished economist, was President of the Royal Statistical

---

* The private owners' wagons of pre-war days (over 500,000) were chiefly confined to coal traffic.

Society, and held 24 doctorates(!). He was consulted by Governments, including Prime Ministers, on important economic problems. Such men enjoyed a prestige and an authority denied to their successors under nationalisation, even such distinguished figures as Sir Brian Robertson and Dr Beeching (both later to be ennobled). The former leaders' salaries, expressed in terms of today's money, were princely. Lord Stamp's £15,000 a year was indeed once criticised at an LMS railway shareholders' meeting, but he adroitly countered (as only an eminent statistician could) by remarking that it represented just the price of one ham sandwich per annum from each shareholder, adding amid laughter 'I am sure you will not grudge me my ham sandwich'.

Chief departmental officers, also well paid by the standards of the day (except perhaps on the LNER) were considerable potentates, sometimes despots, because of the rigid railway pattern of organisation. But the machine worked effectively if sometimes rather clumsily, because it was well understood. There was not the unease that constant upheavals since nationalisation have created, nor the same atmosphere of controversy, since authority had to be respected if careers were to be secure. There was a strong sense of professionalism, maybe sometimes too intolerant of outside or 'amateur' criticism, not unlike that of the armed forces.

And the rank and file railwaymen, though no longer subject to the severe, virtually military discipline enforced in the early days of railways, were nearly all lifelong workers in the industry. Their pay, not brilliant by outside standards, was nevertheless adequate to attract suitable recruits, partly because of the security of the job and minor perquisites such as travel privileges, and in some cases 'tied' or financially assisted housing. In consequence a family feeling existed, above all on the Great Western Railway which had a strong tradition of paternal interest in the welfare of its staff. But the picture was not uniformly rosy; the railway companies' administration was often rather bureaucratic, too much guided by principles and precedent. Rather too often, things were done in a particular way because they had always been done that way and therefore must be right. In particular the personnel side (always 'staff' in those days) was too often liable to work by the book, and to show insufficient latitude or imagination in dealing with individual cases where, as on the LMS, 'staff' work was centralised and largely removed from the control of local departmental managers.

Of more general interest, perhaps, is the comparison of train services between 'then' and 'now'. The period just before nationalisation was not really typical, because of the persisting effects of war-time over-use and under-maintenance. A better comparison, therefore, is with the last halcyon summer before the war, in 1939. A few of the major Inter-City routes are compared below, with Monday to Friday services shown:

Summer timetable. Through services: no change of train

	1939		1984	
	No. of Services	Fastest Time	No of Services	Fastest Time
London–Glasgow				
via Euston	7	6hr 30min	7	5hr 05min
via King's Cross	3	8hr 52min	1	5hr 45min
via St Pancras	3	8hr 38min	no service	
Total	13		8	
London–Edinburgh				
via King's Cross	9	6hr 00min	15	4hr 30min
via St Pancras	3	8hr 40min	no service	
via Euston	2	7hr 05min	no service	
Total	14		15	
London–Aberdeen				
via King's Cross	2	10hr 55min	6	6hr 59min
via Euston	2	12hr 33min	no service	
Total	4		6	
London–Manchester				
via Euston	6	3hr 15min	17	2hr 31min
via St Pancras	9	3hr 35min	no service	
via Marylebone	3	4hr 25min	no service	
Total	18		17	

British Rail After 35 Years

	1939		1984	
	No. of Services	Fastest Time	No. of Services	Fastest Time
London–Liverpool				
via Euston	7	3hr 35min	13	2hr 39min
London–Birmingham				
via Euston	9	1hr 55min	29	1hr 34min
via Paddington	8	2hr 00min	*	*
Total	17			
London–Bristol (TM)				
via Paddington	13	2hr 00min	22+19**	1hr 06min**
London–Exeter St Davids				
via Paddington	7	2hr 50min	15	2hr 03min
via Waterloo	5	3hr 16min	8	3hr 16min†
Total	12		23	
London–Leeds				
via King's Cross	6	3hr 53min	14	2hr 16min
via St Pancras	10	3hr 48min	no service	
Total	16		14	
London–Sheffield				
via St Pancras	10	3hr 05min	13	2hr 20min
via Marylebone	7	3hr 06min	no service	
Total	17		13	
London–Cardiff				
via Paddington	11	2hr 48min	18	1hr 48min

* via Oxford only

** Parkway

† No express service; time is for 13 intermediate calls compared with two calls in 1939 and is to Exeter Central

A comparison of Southern Region services to principal destinations is shown separately in Chapter 5. It is questionable whether any of them can correctly be classed as 'Inter-City'.

Just a handful of selected comparisons cannot be a basis for too sweeping generalisations; but a few things emerge pretty clearly. Today the Inter-City traveller generally enjoys more frequent services and faster services. However, although to Birmingham, say, frequency is much greater, oddly enough to Manchester it is only about the same as pre-war.

Service frequency to several cities has increased substantially on a single route but the total number of trains is often not increased because of the withdrawal of so many services on alternative routes. Improvements in speed are most dramatic over the longest distances, especially on the Anglo-Scottish services. The Western Region shows up well on its three main routes – Bristol, South Wales and the West of England – but does not do so well if the downgrading of many former express services to such cities as Birmingham, Gloucester, Cheltenham, Worcester and Hereford is taken into account, together with the excision of trains to Wolverhampton, Shrewsbury and Chester. The loss of a choice between routes, and the severance of through connections, has a serious total effect upon service quality. 'Through carriages' today are relatively few, as in the search for operational efficiency train sets mostly shuttle between specific destinations – highly convenient for the operators but sometimes involving passengers in changing trains to an extent sufficient to deter them from using rail at all.

Catering services are more frequent on some routes, reduced on others. Buffet services have extensively replaced restaurant cars. Those who argue that this reflects change in popular tastes, and that the pre-war standard table d-hôte meal was due for replacement, should look through the pages of Bradshaw for July 1939 and observe the large range of, for instance, LMS trains on which 'teas and à la carte meals' were offered, and the great range of Pullman services on two of the four companies'

Right:
A reminder of BR at nationalisation, almost twice to-day's network.

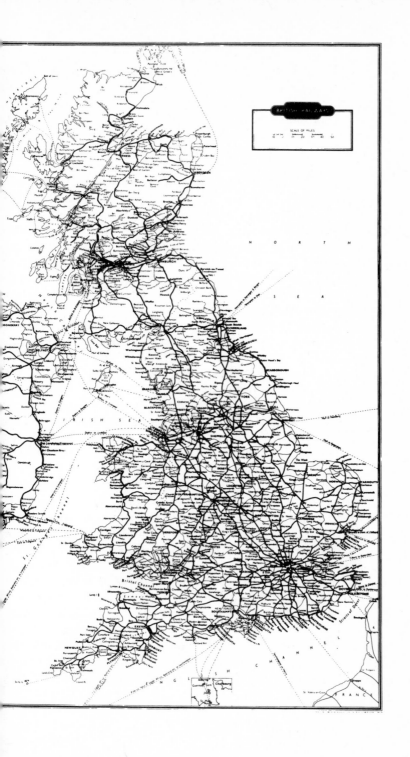

BRITISH RAILWAYS

SCALE OF MILES

trains, providing just the kind of lighter catering allegedly demanded today, *but* to a higher standard than Travellers-Fare can apparently achieve.

In short, there was much more variety and also, perhaps, more glamour about long-distance train travel in 1939. The glamour derived partly from the way in which the principal express trains were presented, with names or destinations displayed on long carriage-roof destination boards – a marketing gimmick that BR unaccountably threw away in the 1960s. The trains were generally clean both outside and in but not always so the locomotives, except on the GWR, and the catering services were usually so popular that restaurant car sittings had to be booked by reservation tickets offered by the chief steward at the start of the journey, something that would gladden the heart of Travellers-Fare today if it were generally the case.

It is hard therefore to analyse just what the traveller has gained and lost overall since 1939. Most people would agree that today's IC 125 High Speed Trains are outstanding for speed, comfort and frequency; yet they are rather standardised and lack the individual character of the earlier named expresses. While their universal provision of some catering is adequate to blunt the pangs of hunger, it is seldom, as it should be, the highlight of a rail journey. (One may except the service of the full English breakfast; while too expensive for the majority of passengers, the standard is excellent.)

On the secondary and branch lines, the modern ubiquitous diesel multiple-unit, in two- and three- or four-car form, is generally an improvement on the former steam-hauled trains of compartment stock, apart perhaps from riding quality, noise and vibration. Speeds are higher, and lighter interiors with better vision all round are a plus point. One may regret the decline of the picturesque country station and its replacement on pay-train routes by austere platforms with minimum shelter, but by and large the now ageing dmu fleet has provided a fair service to the public. What is to replace it seems a question to which BR is still fighting to find the final answer, with four-wheel railbuses, diesel-electric units and as this book goes to press prototype diesel-mechanical units all under trial or small batch production.

For truly revolutionary changes one must look at the freight side. Despite the huge inroads of road transport into the former rail monopoly, the business done in 1939 was still vast. Half a million railway-owned wagons and as many in private ownership trundled about the system in long loose-coupled trains, the banging together of buffers being the most frequent sound wafting away from every important railway line. Anything, virtually, could be sent from anywhere to anywhere – but, how quickly, how regularly, and with what chance of damage? It was these questions that led traders to change so overwhelmingly to road transport, even more than the rate-cutting of which the railways complained so bitterly and which led them to demand total freedom to quote rates in competition with road transport in the so-called 'Square Deal' campaign of 1938–39.

Comparisons with the present are striking: today's selective services of train-load working for individual firms, the highly efficient 'merry-go-round' coal trains shuttling between pitheads and power stations, the Freightliner network, the very limited group of timetabled Speedlink services, are worlds removed from the huge, nation-wide, slow-moving freight traffic of 1939. Looking back provides no worthwhile conclusion – as the Inter-City comparisons do – upon whether there has been real progress in the last 45 years. Freight services have declined in quantity, improved in quality.

So there should be hope for the future, on any reasonable assessment of BR's progress since 1939. Looking at a recent five-year period, surely there is encouragement from these recent improvements in productivity which show that although the 1960s were a period of dramatic change in rail technology and procedures, the impetus has not yet died away.

	1982 as % of 1977
Passenger miles	103
Passenger rolling stock	90
Net tonne miles of freight	87
Freight rolling stock	39
Traction units	84
Staff employed	92
Train miles per staff member	105

What has been the reaction of BR's paymaster, the Government? First, to set pretty unrealistic financial targets for the results of the business; second, to restrict investment to levels which must handicap BR in attracting the revenue required to meet the business targets.

For the year 1984 the authorised levels of investment in the State-owned railways of Europe show Britain in a far lower position than France, West Germany or Italy. Taking traction and rolling stock together with new works (new lines, track upgrading, electrification and signalling) the comparison is:

	Investment in millions of US$	*Route/ Km*
Great Britain	482.72	17,130
France	972.13	34,716
West Germany	1,872.30	28,333
Italy	1,840.33	16,471
Belgium	425.87	3,930
Switzerland (SBB/CFF)	420.64	2,921

Does it make sense to put Britain's railways in the same league as those of Belgium and Switzerland, which have only 23 per cent, and 17 per cent respectively of BR's route-kilometres? Is this the way to exploit a valuable industrial and social asset?

Lastly, does it really help to 'pick out the eyes' of the business, by selling off any profitable subsidiary activities which have contributed net receipts to the BRB as a conglomerate? The result obviously is a further decline in the overall viability of the business as a whole. Is this the undeclared object, to force the public sector to show up badly in comparison with the 'privatised' elements? Admittedly, there may be some arguments in favour of hiving-off activities which are not too effectively managed in a purely rail context. These issues are discussed later, but they pose the query why a suspicious, almost hostile attitude on the part of some Ministers (mainly Conservative) and some civil servants (officially non-party) has grown up. At the same time, BR has suffered not merely from Government apathy or criticism but also from a few self-inflicted wounds, inflicted, one must stress, from the best of motives as a rule! BR's record is complex and over-simplified conclusions should be avoided, even by politicians and journalists – though that may be asking too much!

2

Men at the Top, and Reorganisation Fever

It would not be too strong to say that the chairmanship of BR has often proved to be a frustrating position even though it is of exalted status. All the chairmen have been men of distinction who laboured hard to make a contribution to BR's fortunes; it was sad that some of them left with feelings of disappointment or irritation. All, however, felt that they had been well supported by their Board colleagues and chief officers; it was external rather than internal forces that led to frustration. But why?

One should perhaps look first at the way in which the appointments of chairmen have been made. In the first spate of nationalisation Acts of Parliament passed by the Labour Government of 1945–51, a huge range of top jobs in the public sector was rapidly created. It was believed, rather naïvely, that the very fact that they were in the public sector would attract men of the highest calibre, and that salaries therefore could be fixed more in relation to the scales prevailing for top posts in the civil service than to those in major industries. The first Chairman of the Railway Executive, Sir Eustace Missenden, was paid £7,000, which was less than one-half the salary that had been paid to Lord Stamp as President of the London Midland and Scottish Railway although that railway had only been about one-third of the size of British Railways after nationalisation.

The professional railwaymen mostly accepted this downgrading of prospects because they were committed to a railway career, though a minority moved out into private industry. But when Governments imagined that a solution to

BR's financial problems could be found through importing outside business talent, things became difficult. It was discovered that Dr Richard Beeching was paid £24,000 a year as Technical Director of Imperial Chemical Industries and was, quite naturally, unwilling to take a cut in salary if he accepted the pressing invitation of the then Minister, Ernest Marples, to become Chairman of the British Transport Commission initially and, shortly after, of the British Railways Board. But this salary, when it became public, created a hullabaloo that only showed what an unrealistic view had been taken of the nationalised industries. Dr Beeching's appointment was a break-through and most subsequent nominations to the BRB were accompanied by more flexibility over remuneration. Even so, Ministerial first choices were not always easily lured away from richer pastures. The position carried few perquisites other than free rail travel, and the subservience to Ministers which steadily increased as BR's financial position worsened could be very unpalatable. Hardly anyone who has held the chairmanship can have retired with a feeling of achievement and satisfaction, except possibly the astute Sir Henry Johnson whose career was always marked by his flair for being in the right place at the right time, but never staying too long. Even such outstanding figures as Sir Brian (Lord) Robertson and Dr (Lord) Beeching left in a mood of some dissatisfaction. The lively spirit of Richard (Lord) Marsh led him to express his views pointedly; his successor, Sir Peter Parker, used more diplomatic phraseology through which nevertheless his feelings peeped out.

The position of chairman has been an equivocal one. Apart from the incumbent at the time of writing, only three out of eight had been professional railwaymen (Sir Stanley Raymond came late into the railway field). The others were unable to enter into railway management in the way that a pre-nationalisation general manager could do, by drawing upon a wide and deep experience of the railway and its working that was usually superior to that of the departmental chiefs putting forward proposals for approval. The distinguished outsiders, who included two men from big business, one soldier and one politician-cum-business expert, had to form their judgments without the confidence imparted by a professional background.

Hence they could be over-persuaded on occasion by the technical experts or, for that matter, by regional managements. Sir Brian Robertson, for instance, an outstanding administrator of the utmost integrity and ability, endorsed various features of the 1955 modernisation plan which time has shown to be misconceived – the marshalling yards programme, the multiplication of diesel locomotive types, and the standardisation of the vacuum brake for mineral wagons are among them.

Different chairmen have nevertheless been personally associated in the public mind with some aspect or other of railway progress. Sir Brian was identified with the modernisation plan of 1955; Dr Beeching with Re-shaping (or closures in layman's terms) and the emergence of the Freightliner concept; Sir Henry Johnson with the completion of the first major main line electrification and the reconstruction of Euston Station; Richard (Lord) Marsh with the development of the Advanced Passenger Train in prototype form.

But there has been a constant underlying Government pressure to relieve the taxpayer of all responsibility for maintaining rail services, which seemed to stem from a belief that the railways could resume the position of financial viability, albeit rather precarious, which they had enjoyed before nationalisation. There was an obstinate and unrealistic refusal to accept the need for a new look at the railways in post-war Britain which was moving ever more rapidly into the motor age. No such difficulty existed on the Continent, especially in France and Germany, where railways were regarded as an essential part of the national infrastructure; railway deficits were accepted as a necessary consequence of the need for comprehensive nation-wide transport services. Nationalisation had of course existed longer in these countries, and the funds required were provided almost as unquestioningly as those needed for electricity supply or water supply. Also, the railways' top echelons enjoyed considerable influence in Government circles, especially with senior civil servants. In France this was not unconnected with the fact that many senior railway managers were in the charmed circle of former 'Polytechniciens', the club or stable from which the French 'establishment' is so largely recruited.

By contrast, in Britain, with its long tradition of private enterprise in transport, the nationalised railways were always a favourite target of press and parliamentary criticism from the right, without their managements enjoying corresponding support from the left. All this made life difficult enough for the chairmen, striving to present a good public image of the railways and also to preserve good personal relations with Ministers, a task often exacerbated by changes of Government or of individual Ministers during a chairman's term of office. This meant that a chairman appointed by one political party with a remit to manage the railways on lines favoured by that party, might suddenly find a new Minister calling a halt to a policy that was just beginning to gather momentum. That certainly befell Dr Beeching: he was appointed by Ernest Marples in May 1961 with a remit to adopt draconian measures if necessary to put BR into financial viability; he published the 'Re-shaping' report in March 1963 but its proposals were only just taking effect when in October 1964 the Government fell and the brake was put on, with the result that in May 1965 Dr Beeching returned (with a peerage) to ICI.

His predecessor, Sir Brian (Lord) Robertson, had had to deal with no fewer than four Ministers: A. T. Lennox-Boyd, J. Boyd-Carpenter, Harold Watkinson, and Ernest Marples. It was perhaps helpful to him that they all came from the same party. But John Elliot had dealt with Alfred Barnes (Labour), J. S. Maclay (Liberal-Conservative) and Lennox-Boyd (Conservative), all in the space of two years and four months! Richard (Lord) Marsh dealt with John Peyton (Conservative), Fred Mulley and John Gilbert (Labour).

It may be appropriate to contrast the personalities of the chairmen up to the mid-1970s. The first Chairman of BR, Sir Eustace Missenden, was actually only the head of the Railway Executive, over which the British Transport Commission exercised theoretical control. It was theoretical largely because Alfred Barnes, the Minister who had carried through the nationalisation Act had insisted upon personally appointing the chairman and members of the Executive as well as those of the Commission. This was largely responsible for the Executive members declining to consider themselves as merely agents of the Commission, though contacts with the Ministry had to be through the BTC as a matter of protocol. Missenden should perhaps have been grateful for being insulated from the Minister and his civil servants because, although he was an experienced and practical railwayman, he did not move easily in the world of politics, and he did not impress either politicians or civil servants. He made no secret of his dislike of the whole organisation and his relations with Sir Cyril (Lord) Hurcomb, the Chairman of the Commission, were far from cordial.

Missenden was successful in fending off the BTC's impatience at the slow progress being made with the 'integration' required by the 1947 Transport Act, and also its disquiet about the programme of building new standard steam locomotives. His successor, (Sir) John Elliot was much more co-operative and also much more of a political animal. The son of a famous editor of the *Daily Express*, he knew such public figures as Lord Beaverbrook, and his relations with the Commission were handled skilfully. Had the Executive's demise not loomed ahead for the greater part of his two years in office, he would probably have made a very significant contribution to planning a modernised railway system.

Elliot's contacts with the Minister (Lennox-Boyd), whom the Conservative Government had placed in charge of the Bill to abolish the Railway Executive and de-nationalise road haulage, were largely concerned with the question of Elliot's own future after the body over which he presided had disappeared; that problem was solved by the resignation of Lord Latham, Chairman of London Transport, prompted by the Government's appointment of a Committee of Inquiry into London Transport, which left a vacancy for Elliot to fill.

The 1953 Act put the British Transport Commission in direct charge of the railways, apart from the functions decentralised to area authorities. The Commission also absorbed the functions of the other Executives (apart from London Transport) which had been created by the 1947 Act. So the new Chairman, Sir Brian Robertson, reported to be Winston Churchill's personal choice, had to exercise a dual role as chief executive of the railways and also chairman of the whole complex of nationalised transport, road haulage, docks, inland waterways, buses, hotels and rail catering. If this task was formidable, so was the man. Sir Brian, tall, austere, given to prolonged silences where other men would have indulged in small talk, was universally respected, admired by many and feared by some. Only the small number who worked very closely with him were aware of a human side to his character and could add affection to respect; but for the most part he remained aloof and Olympian, something of a legendary figure. His formal presentation of any case, either orally or in writing, was always masterly. But in the $7\frac{1}{2}$ years in which he presided over BR the slide into deficit which started in 1955 caused ever-increasing concern to the Government. Two investigations – one by the House of Commons Select Committee on Nationalised Industries, the other by an unofficial group chaired by (Sir) Ivan Stedeford, a leading industrialist, reporting direct to the Minister of Transport – were heavily critical of the whole set-up. The Select Committee was deeply impressed by the evidence given by Sir Brian and said so in its Report. But in the end, this distinguished soldier and administrator retired in an atmosphere of denigration that was undeserved. He had worked immensely hard at an impossible task and some have suggested that this shortened his life, even though a peerage made perhaps some amends for his rather shabby treatment.

His successor, Dr Richard Beeching, had been a member of the Stedeford advisory group and in this capacity had struck the Minister, Ernest Marples, as just the man to put BR's finances right. His task was made easier in some respects than that of his predecessor, since the huge unwieldy structure of the BTC was to be broken up into its main constituents, each under a board reporting direct to the Minister. Dr Beeching's remit, however, was just as unrealistic as that given to Sir Brian Robertson, in that he was expected very quickly to find a solution to the complex problem of financial viability for the railways. The Beeching approach was on the face of it entirely logical. In the huge mass of operations conducted by the railways, although the overall results showed a loss, there was a shortage of information as to just which operations and which parts of the system made a loss, which broke even, and which made a profit. He set on foot a huge costing exercise designed to pin-point the areas of loss and profit; the result was the 'Re-shaping' report which exploded in the Press as a horror story. To the Minister it appeared fully to justify his faith in Dr Beeching, even though the political backlash prevented anything like full impementation of the drastic proposals in the Report for closures and service withdrawals; there were far too many which affected marginal constituencies!

Dr Beeching suffered the experience of other chairmen of BR, in that a political change and the need to work with a new Minister took place before his policies had time to be given real effect. He had taken up the chairmanship in June 1961, only seven months after Ernest Marples had become Minister. The Re-shaping report was printed in March 1963, and its counterpart document, *The Development of the Major Trunk Routes*, in February 1965. But the sensation caused by the first paper had scarcely died away, and a start made with implementing some of its less controversial (and less politically sensitive) proposals, when, in October 1964, the Conservative Government fell and Beeching found himself dealing with a Labour Minister of Transport, Tom Fraser, who could scarcely be expected to bless the Marples/Beeching policies. Beeching thereupon returned to ICI in May 1965.

His successor (Sir) Stanley Raymond, had been his Vice-Chairman and a trusted supporter. Raymond's temperament was very different from that of the calm, relaxed, cigar-smoking Beeching. He was energetic and impatient, and frequently adopted an abrasive manner which could upset people; yet no one could fail to admire the way in which, starting as an orphan with no family advantages, he had fought his way to the top by sheer hard work and ability. His very abrasiveness no doubt stemmed from a continuing tendency to see life in terms of a struggle. Once convinced of the rightness of a policy, he would pursue it with almost religious fervour; any opposition or hesitation in executing it seemed to him like heresy. He found it difficult to delegate with confidence that work would be done exactly as he wished; this made him a rather 'untidy administrator', as one of his closest aides commented.

It was perceptive of Beeching, in giving a farewell talk to his chief officers, to say that he himself had had a flying start from his originally close relationship with the then Minister; such an advantage would not necessarily be enjoyed by Raymond.

Beeching therefore asked his officers to give his successor the fullest and most loyal support, which he might well need. These were prophetic words. Raymond was, like Beeching, to find that a change of Ministers made life difficult for a chairman. The amiable Tom Fraser, the Labour Minister who had appointed Raymond, was replaced in December 1965 by the able and determined Mrs Barbara Castle.

It was ironical that Raymond should force the premature retirement of one of the most brilliant and perceptive railwaymen of his generation, Gerard Fiennes, in consequence of what most people would consider a quite minor indiscretion in his fascinating autobiography. The irony lay in the fact that Raymond, after a strong disagreement with the fiery Mrs Castle on policy, should himself be forced to 'relinquish his appointment' in December 1967.

No such fate befell the shrewd, affable career railwayman who succeeded Raymond, Sir Henry ('Bill') Johnson. He indeed was the chief beneficiary of the breathing-space afforded to BR by the financial restructuring under Mrs Castle's 1968 Transport Act. He retired in September 1971 with his reputation further enhanced rather than impaired, having been the residuary legatee of the last and richest fruits of the 1955 Modernisation Plan such as the London Midland main line electrification, the completion of the new Euston Station, and the Southern Region electrification to Southampton and Bournemouth.

There was more irony, in that for some 18 months Johnson dealt (usually amicably) with Mrs Castle's successor at the Ministry, Richard Marsh, who eventually, after a period in business consultancy, was in September 1971 to be his successor at BRB headquarters. An interesting change of roles, an ex-Labour Minister of Transport being appointed Chairman of BR by his Conservative successor at the Ministry!

There could hardly be three more different personalities than Raymond, Johnson and Marsh. Raymond was dedicated, hard-working, a strange combination of the ruthless and the emotional. Johnson delegated extensively to those he could trust, usually those coming from the same stable as himself. Friendly in manner, he nevertheless was always watchful for trouble ahead that might require quick evasive action. His outwardly easy approach and relaxed manner masked the fact that he was actually highly strung; few would guess how much he needed to nerve himself for an important occasion or how thoroughly he would brief himself for a tricky interview with a politician. Marsh on the other hand seemed highly extrovert; relaxed, witty, quick to seize a point, amusingly self-deprecating and yet keeping a sharp eye on the main issues. His staff soon got used to having a television and radio personality as their chief; he never lost an opportunity of putting the railway case effectively through the media. At times he seemed to get weary of endlessly arguing with a rather unresponsive Ministry over investment, and his comments verged on the caustic, which did not always endear him to his own former officials in the Ministry at No 2 Marsham Street, Westminster, though his relations with the Conservative Minister, John Peyton, were good – better than with Peyton's Labour successor, Fred Mulley, which was another irony!

The important question that must be asked is whether a chairman of BR can shape policy and determine events; does it in fact matter tremendously who is appointed, provided he can chair a Board meeting and subsequently put forward the consensus view of the Board? History certainly shows that Missenden gave the functional members of the Railway Executive a free hand within their own functions, with rather unhappy results. On the other hand, Sir Brian Robertson in his Olympian way certainly took decisions; his training had taught him that the commander-in-chief must never seem indecisive! That these decisions were by no means always right was not due to shortcomings on his part, because he always weighed up the evidence presented to him carefully. What he lacked was railway professional 'hunch', where the evidence was incomplete or possibly misleading.

Dr Beeching, too, certainly took decisions and defended them brilliantly, even where the supporting evidence was really inadequate. Some other chairmen however seem to have concentrated upon the public relations aspect of their position, (sometimes very effectively) and have left the internal decisions rather too completely to the professionals.

This of course raises the question of whether the railways need have a chief executive concerned with internal management, leaving the chairman free to concentrate on external relations. Beeching allowed his vice-chairman Philip Shirley to assume something of this role, but without the formal title. Since then, chief executives have come and gone in an often uneasy re-adjustment of responsibilities. Sometimes the post has been combined with that of vice-chairman or deputy chairman of the Board; sometimes it has not carried with it Board membership. Willie Thorpe, an extrovert and successful railwayman, held the dual role for a time but relinquished the position of chief executive on the grounds that he was thereby responsible to himself as vice-chairman, which was a nonsense.

To be effectively chairman *and* chief executive of the railways is arguably too heavy a burden for anyone, though the undaunted Sir Brian told the Select Committee that he discharged it, not merely for the railways, but for all forms of nationalised transport. The Committee was sceptical about the practicability of effective combination of the two roles.

It is perhaps relevant that the Board of the former LMS composed mainly of experienced businessmen, concluded that that railway, although in many ways smaller than BR today, was too big to be under a single General Manager and transferred the work of that post to an Executive Committee of Vice-Presidents under a President of the Executive.

At the time of writing, (1985) the BR Headquarters organisation is a compromise between a 'chief executive' pattern and a 'functional Board' pattern. Below the chairman, deputy chairman and vice-chairman, there are eight members, to four of whom departmental 'reporting lines' are shown. But the 'railway business' which in the past has been sometimes managed and co-ordinated by a single chief executive is headed, in the BRB's own words, by a triumvirate comprising the Head of the business (the Chairman) and two Joint Managing Directors on the Board. Overall control is exercised by the triumvirate operating flexibly, as the need arises. In fact, the two Managing Directors share between them control of the 'Line' Departments of the railway – one group comprising engineering and operations, the other commercial matters in the widest sense. 'Staff' functions have reporting lines to the Chairman, Vice-Chairman and one Member.

A solution, perhaps a better one, that is widely adopted in

other European countries is that of the two-tier Board. There is a superior body ('Conseil d'Administration' or 'Verwaltungs-rat') of entirely part-time members, usually under the chairmanship of a distinguished non-railwayman; and a lower full-time executive Board ('Comité de Gérance' or 'Vorstand') of professionals headed by a chairman who is like the LMS President. The roles of the two bodies are quite distinct and well understood. The superior body deals with Government policy, budgets and economics; the lower body is the effective management of the railways. There is much to be said for this separation of functions, because a wide range of outside contacts, talent and experience can be drawn upon, with representation of major interests such as labour and transport users, on the superior Board. Its status vis-à-vis the Government can be good when its chairman is a distinguished figure, who need not have expertise in the details of railway work. Meanwhile the post of chief executive is made less burdensome by being carried by a group of functional specialists, though the chief executive is the channel of contact with the superior Board. It works well in France and Germany: why not here?

Lastly, is it not time that the practice of appointing chairmen for five years only was revised? (In fact, the average tenure of office by chairmen since nationalisation has been around four years only.) The outstanding railway leaders before nationalisation – Stamp, Wedgwood, Walker, Milne – were in office for around 15 years in most cases, and they were learning all the time. If Ministers are confident that they have made the right choice, appointments should surely be until retiring age, subject only to the right of the Minister to terminate an appointment in the unlikely event of inefficiency or misconduct.

During the three and a half decades since nationalisation, the railways have seen more changes in their management structures than took place in all their previous history. One would have thought that the fusion of four great companies into a single corporation under public ownership would have led to a finally settled organisation pattern, smoothing out the differences that formerly existed between the four companies, and standardising the most effective procedures. Far from it. Change has been almost continuous, sometimes enforced by legislative measures, sometimes initiated within BR itself. Is this last a sign of lively, adaptable thinking, or is it due to other motives, such as a desire to escape from less soluble problems?

Most railway managers in the middle or junior ranges would probably agree that the disruption caused by re-organisation ('when you re-organise us, we bleed' as Gerry Fiennes perceptively remarked) has gone far to cancel out the benefits. Once the decision to change has been taken, there is usually a freeze upon filling posts that fall vacant; this may last many months, meanwhile creating much difficulty in carrying on with routine duties. Then there is (usually) opposition from the Trades Unions to overcome, which may absorb a great deal of time and energy. (This is inevitable when the declared intention of the changes is to reduce administrative costs and hence the number of staff.) Meanwhile most people are worrying about their personal future in ways that distract them from effective concentration on daily tasks. The grapevine becomes active and rumours circulate. Jockeying for position and lobbying take place right up to the date of the changeover. The costs of the changeover are usually considerable. New office accommodation may have to be built, purchased or rented. The physical removals can be disruptive; where managers and staff have to move their homes, they can be pre-occupied with domestic matters to the detriment of their official duties.

Once the new organisation has been introduced, some will enjoy more authority but others feel downgraded and embittered. Ascertaining the exact limits of authority and the new relationships with colleagues takes time. And the theoretical savings from a reduction in the number of established posts are slow to be reflected in the cash flow. Redundancies can be costly, and the energetic exercise of self-interest while the new machinery is being set up can often result in more posts, or more highly graded ones, being established than was envisaged when the plan was first put forward.

All this sounds rather pessimistic. Replanning the organisation may yield some benefits or even be necessary on occasions. But railway work falls into a few definite groups and, for over a century, organisation patterns based on them have evolved. In the very early days the secretary and the engineer were the principal officers, with the directors carrying out functions later entrusted to management. But it was not long before the four

We shall soon have forgotten the magnificence (and the muddle) of the old Euston . . . *(Crown Copyright: National Railway Museum)*

. . . being used to its efficient if rather characterless replacement *(Author)*

The trick of designing smooth-riding stock like this seemed for a while to have eluded the engineers – until Mark III arrived *(British Rail)*

Smooth and sleek; the Victoria–Gatwick trains are the envy of the commuters of Brighton! *(Author)*

chief departments or functions – maintaining the way and works, providing and maintaining motive power and rolling stocks, obtaining traffic, and organising the movement of trains – emerged, with a simple line of authority from chief departmental officers to district officers, and, below them, to local officers – stationmasters, goods agents, yardmasters, shedmasters, area engineers, and so on.

Of course, the need for cross-links below the top level existed, to avoid the need for the general manager's organisation to coordinate the functional departments. The Great Western Railway had an area officer for South Wales, the London Midland & Scottish a chief officer for Scotland. This went some way to recognise the need for these links in areas remote from the central management. The most thorough exercise of decentralised authority was of course on the London & North Eastern Railway with its three divisional general managers below the chief general manager.

Now if the LNER organisation had been adopted on British Railways at nationalisation, instead of the rather rigid departmentalism of the Railway Executive, probably much of the friction between the Executive and the Regions that existed from 1948 to 1953 would have been avoided.

The upheaval of the latter year, due to the Transport Act, 1953, was only the first of many reorganisations. Those who lived through it at the headquarters of the British Transport Commission can testify to the confusion that was caused and lasted for months until Sir Brian Robertson issued his famous 'Grey Book' describing the new organisation which he intended, of course, to be permanent, after it had been approved by the Minister. It was a masterpiece of misplaced ingenuity involving BR in a tangle of non-railway bodies at headquarters. A regional general manager's submission to the BTC might have to run the gauntlet of the British Railways Central Staff, Area Board, General Staff of the Commission, Railways Sub-Commission, Committee of the Commission, and, finally, the Commission itself.

This organisation was never fully understood except perhaps at the very top level. Meanwhile the regions carried on much as before as regards internal organisation but enjoying more autonomy through the operation of area boards, with (limited) delegated powers of managerial control and from Sir Brian Robertson's careful observance of the Government's desire that the regions should be treated rather more like the former railway companies. However, the restless, enquiring mind of Sir Reginald Wilson became dissatisfied with the pattern that he encountered on the Eastern Region after becoming Chairman of the Eastern Area Board. He produced the concept of the 'Line' structure which worked admirably largely in the Eastern Region because it was founded upon the company structure that had evolved slowly and naturally, without interference from Government or anybody else, up to the grouping of 1923 – which was a misconceived measure, though designed by an ex-railway manager (Sir Eric Geddes) turned Cabinet Minister.

Rather sadly, after the huge unwieldy BTC was split up and the British Railways Board created by the Transport Act of 1962, the 'Line' concept gradually died and was replaced by large traffic and engineering divisions with geographical boundaries replacing former districts, with (allegedly) savings in total staff numbers. Operational management based on systems was now subjected to purely geographical boundaries which produced some oddities. For example, on the former Southern Region line from Salisbury to Exeter, Crewkerne was looked after by the Western Region Area Manager at Westbury, with which Crewkerne had no train connections at all.

The divisional concept meant that some traffic offices in quite important centres, that had been quite recently created in order to bring local managers into closer touch with their customers, were now closed. Great Eastern House at Cambridge for instance was sold and staff were transferred, lock stock and barrel, to Norwich.

The size of the divisions can be envisaged from the fact that there were only three for the whole Western Region. Scotland eventually merged region and divisions, by a two-tier organisation which ran direct to Area Managers. Areas were of course larger than the former stations or depots and problems arose of maintaining the local contacts that the stationmaster had had, with considerable if inconspicuous benefits to the railway.

But the pressure was on to reduce administrative costs. In 1958 a scheme was worked out for separating the bi-regional departments shared between the Eastern and North Eastern Regions, an arrangement which had involved much wasteful correspondence and travelling. This task was completed, but only seven years later a proposal was approved by the BRB to amalgamate the Eastern and North Eastern regions, on the grounds of cost and efficiency. So into reverse everything went!

The change of Government in 1964 made inevitable the production of yet another Transport Act, and yet another look at organisation. The Act in fact required the BRB to report on this subject to the Minister. But a Joint Steering Committee of the BRB – joint between the Ministry and the Board – had already proposed a new form of organisation placing more emphasis upon the divisions, with a suggestion that in this context the abolition of regions might be considered. Consultants (Cooper Bros) had been consulted and favoured a continuance of regions for the time being but ultimately envisaged a two-tier management structure below the BRB in which the lower tier would comprise geographical management units larger than the divisions, but probably smaller than the regions. They also wanted a chief executive for the railways, something that the BRB (like the BTC before it) had shied away from.

Having digested all these reports, the Minister (Barbara Castle) put into the 1968 Act a requirement to get her approval to a scheme of organisation. The Board tried to ensure that this would be done in ways that she would approve by engaging McKinsey & Co Inc as consultants. McKinsey was a name to conjure with but it could be doubted whether its consultants ever fully appreciated the complex interworking of the railway system. Their reports read well and plausibly, but the separation of the 'businesses' and the appointment of executive directors (more recently transformed into Sector Directors, but *plus ça change . . .*) is somewhat artificial, as is the book-keeping which tries to produce 'results' for the 'businesses'. However, the need for a chief executive who would be neither the chairman nor the deputy chairman was stressed by McKinsey, and for a time accepted by the BRB.

McKinsey consultants and a team of railway officers

thereafter jointly produced the Field Organisation Report, which envisaged the abolition of regions and their replacement by eight 'Territories', with Service Group Managements traversing territory boundaries. Three years were estimated to be necessary for the implementation of this change; in the event, it being bitterly opposed by the trades unions, the BRB suddenly abandoned it after a vast amount of preliminary work had been carried out and many posts had been frozen for so long as to cause acute staffing problems.

But the desire to reorganise, to be seen to be doing *something*, reappeared with the Sector Management idea, revamping the Executive Directorates under Inter-City, Freight, Parcels, London & South East and Provincial headings. At the time of writing, the latest organisational structure is described as 'two-tier', since, by abolishing divisions, regions are working directly to areas as has long been the practice in Scotland. Much work has been involved in planning the changeover and cushioning some of its more painful consequences.

What can one make of this apparently endless debate, these constant permutations of more, or less, centralisation; of functional or non-functional Boards; of executive or non-executive chairmen; of large divisions or no divisions; of large areas or small areas? If one were cynical, one might suggest that reorganisation planning, drawing charts or family trees on paper and engaging consultants may be a form of escape from the grinding hard work involved in keeping the standards of service acceptable, in the face of inadequate investment and unco-operative trades unions. The pendulum seems to swing pretty regularly; but those who give it a push can feel that they have achieved something, if only for a short time. Moreover it is a useful ploy for a Transport Minister to be able to answer criticisms, either of BR or of his own record in regard to the railways, by saying that he has demanded a reorganisation that should improve 'efficiency and economy' (that meaningless phrase beloved of the civil service).

It can be argued that organisations, above all in railways, must be left to mature before their weaknesses calling for action can be identified. Pulling the plant up by the roots every few years inhibits growth and causes severe flagging of the foliage, even if it eventually recovers. A fair proportion of the changes since 1948 have done as much harm as good to BR's efficiency. From this must be excepted the short-lived Line organisation on the Eastern Region, which worked admirably and should never have been replaced by the divisional structure.

What about the round of changes that banished the Western Region's headquarters to Swindon, with the London Midland following to Birmingham? A cynic may whisper that if it is desired to slim down the managerial and administrative staff, there is nothing like a long-distance office removal to provoke a spate of voluntary early retirements! But that is not a very selective process.

In principle the move to a two-tier, region – area, managerial structure seems well justified. Again the cynic could comment that new areas look very much like the old districts, abolished when the divisions were set up 20 years ago, under another name. And an area manager has been appointed for Cornwall with extended powers, and the brand name 'Cornwall Railway' has been used for publicity purposes. Shades of the London, Tilbury & Southend Line of 1957! Is there nothing new in the railway world? Whether the standard of service will improve is much more important than whether the two-tier organisation shows savings in staff and office overheads compared with divisions. The crucial point is the focussing of authority within the area manager's patch. With most of his train services originating or terminating in other areas, what control can he exercise and just what can he do at station, depot, and signalbox level? The disappearance of the stationmaster has had many side-effects, some of them undesirable; there is a chance now to rectify them. Stations that seldom see the 'guv'nor' during the morning commuter peak, and never in the evening peak after 5pm, are potential points of danger and lost business. The railway does not run from 9 to 5 and office hours do not suit it at grass roots level.

A question must hang over the relationship of Sectors with Regions. Business theory has long recognised three main methods of devolution, ie of chains of authority. They are, by function; by territory; and by product. BR has tried, sometimes voluntarily and sometimes under political pressure, all three systems. The Railway Executive of 1948–53 under the 1947 Act used the functional system; its disadvantages led to the 1953 Transport Act which stressed territorial devolution, ie to Regional general management. Since the mid-1960s there has been a prolonged attempt to devolve on a product basis.

Today there is obviously a potential clash between Sector management (devolution by product) and Regional management (devolution by territory). The existence of two chains of devolved authority is not unknown in business, at any rate where 'Line' and 'Staff' organisation principles are followed. One must therefore ask whether Sectors are 'Staff' and Regions 'Line' – and is this distinction clearly laid down and understood?

It is usually the case that few managers are content with a planning or 'staff' role – they itch to command the resources needed to achieve the results they predicate. However if Sectors concentrate upon planning, setting targets and upon quality control monitoring, with Regions as the 'line' management concentrating upon what may be termed the supply side, an organisational clash need not be envisaged. It may be tempting to draw charts and write out new job specifications, but BR has suffered from so many upheavals (above all the imposed Field organisation which ended in fiasco) that a period of consolidation with concentration on detailed improvements is vastly preferable to sweeping changes. Most organisations can be made to work if they are well understood and there is a spirit of cooperation. If the latter is absent, even the theoretically ideal organisation will not work. It is perhaps worth concluding this chapter with a couplet by Alexander Pope:

> 'For forms of government let fools contest,
> Whate'er is best administered is best.'

3

The Engineers and their Priorities

The status and role of the civil engineer in the railways have always been rather special. He is in the line of descent from Stephenson, Brunel, and Locke, and all the other great men who used to be entitled, simply, 'the Engineer', who laid out our basic railway system. Even today, each new civil engineer appointed to the Western Region is ceremonially presented with Brunel's walking stick, with its ingenious aids to surveying which the illustrious builder of the GWR took with him on his countless journeys. More significantly, perhaps, the RCE still retains some relics of the authority exerted by his predecessors. In the team of regional departmental officers, he is often still able to lay down standards which are less easily questioned than the policies of his colleagues, partly because he can always play the trump card, his responsibility for the safety of the line.

All BR's civil engineers have been, and still are, highly professional, dedicated to their task of keeping the railway running at all times. Most have also been interested in new techniques and have been free from ultra-conservatism. But nowadays the alarming cost of maintaining the railway infrastructure is a major factor that weakens the competitive power of railways in relation to the opposition, mainly the roads. It is a fact that the great inherent economy of movement in train-loads instead of car-loads or lorry-loads is partially nullified by the heavy and rather inflexible costs of maintaining the infrastructure.

So the engineer is no longer immune from being cross-examined on every aspect of his procedures and cost levels. In the maintenance of permanent way, there have been steady moves towards the mechanisation of what had traditionally been a very labour-intensive function, due partly to the standardisation of continuous welded rail with concrete sleepers and 'Pandrol' fastenings, partly to the application of machines to replace hand labour, starting with power ballast cleaners and tampers, and progressing to the modern Plasser-Theurer and Cowan-Sheldon equipment for tracklaying. Changes in switch design, the development of high-speed turnouts, and sequential single crossovers replacing double crossovers, together with reversible working facilities, are all evidence of a progressive outlook.

In the major structural works carried out since nationalisation, the civil engineers have a considerable number of achievements to their credit – the rebuilding of Euston and major stations at Birmingham New Street, Coventry and elsewhere in connection with the London Midland electrification; the rebuilding of Stephenson's Britannia Bridge; on the Southern Region the reconstruction of Cannon Street, Holborn Viaduct and Blackfriars stations are all notable projects.

However, the traditional independence of the civil engineer needs to be tempered by the oversight by general management which, while not interfering in purely technical standards, must hold the balance between departmental policies. Two contrasting episodes from past history may illustrate this. One is the celebrated case of the River class express passenger locomotives designed for the former Highland Railway by its Locomotive Engineer, F. G. Smith. He had unfortunately failed to consult the Chief Engineer, Alexander Newlands, about their design, and the axle-loadings were found to exceed the limits laid down by the Civil Engineer. But Smith had paid particular attention to the balancing of moving parts and he claimed that the stresses on track and bridges from hammer-blow effect were actually less than those from locomotives with lower nominal axle-loadings.

Newlands however placed an absolute ban on the use of these engines. The General Manager and the Board felt unable to over-rule him; so Smith was sacked, and the locomotives – a splendid class, badly needed by the traffic department – were sold to the Caledonian Railway. The irony of the story is that in later years, when the Highland and the Caledonian had both been swept up into the new LMS, the River class engines returned to the Highland line where they performed with great efficiency, after a relatively trifling expenditure had been incurred on some local bridge strengthening. Management had failed in this case to take hold properly. Smith should no doubt have been reprimanded for his failure to consult Newlands. (It was notorious that these two gentlemen did not get on well but that should not have been allowed to continue to the company's detriment.) And Newlands' ban should have been subject to a review by outside engineering consultants, who would have shown how the River class could have been permitted to run, after some quite minor engineering work had been carried out.

The second episode shows management in just the opposite sense, doing exactly what it ought to do in a crisis. Curiously enough, it was another River class of locomotive that was involved – Maunsell's 2–6–4 tank engines – one of which was derailed with a fast train near Sevenoaks, killing 13 passengers. Maunsell maintained that the track must have been at fault; George Ellson, the chief engineer, insisted that the design of the locomotive must be the reason. Sir Herbert Walker, the General Manager, listened to both sides carefully and then directed, first that this class of locomotive should be withdrawn from traffic and converted to tender engines, and, second, that the main line in question should be reballasted throughout to improve its condition for fast running. One engine of the class was even tried out for stability on the Great Northern main line and was found to ride far better than on the SEC route Nobody was sacked and nobody won the argument. That was management at its best.

In recent years the civil engineers have, as mentioned above, carried out many notable tasks and greatly modernised their procedures. But one cannot refrain from some small criticisms. First, untidiness! All along the track there lie large quantities of civil engineering débris – crop-ends of rails, old iron castings, sleepers, tubing, fishplates and so on. The total value, even at scrap prices, of all this material, mainly iron and steel, must be considerable. Moreover it invites vandalism, and has brought comment from the Chief Inspecting Officer of Railways of the Department of Transport.

No doubt it will be argued that collection involves expense, and is difficult if not impossible while the line is under traffic. But surely, at the end of every engineer's possession, it should be a responsibility of those concerned to remove all discarded materials, which have after all been brought there at some time or other. And as for the material that already lies around, the traffic people might concede a possession in the small hours of the night in order that a locomotive with a few flat wagons and a riding van equipped with a searchlight could take a gang, stopping whenever required, to retrieve this lineside débris, before normal traffic resumes.

The great John Miller, Engineer of the LNER's North Eastern Area, was something of a fanatic about 'good housekeeping' methods along the track. He instituted neat concrete edging at junctions to contain the ballast and insisted upon collection of all scrap and rubbish, much of which was sorted at a Central Reclamation Depot at Darlington, a surprising quantity becoming available for re-use or sale as scrap. We could do with a few John Millers today in a number of Civil Engineering Areas.

There is another matter that receives scant attention but which contributes perhaps unfairly, to a rather poor public impression of BR – the filth (paper, tins, bottles, and less mentionable stuff) that can be seen on the ballast between the platforms at terminal stations, even though the public is usually responsible, if indirectly, for it being there. Sometimes, but rarely, staff of the chief civil engineer can be seen trying to pick up this litter by hand: usually it remains for weeks or months on end. Surely an answer is there: terminal tracks should be laid on concrete slab or be asphalted. They can then be hosed down or swept out quickly and cheaply.

Another regrettable practice that has grown up in recent years is that of discharging old dirty ballast to the side of the track, instead of removing it in the wagons that have brought new ballast to the site. Presumably this is a cost-cutting exercise; but where will it end after two or three ballast renewals? And for what purpose was all the investment in those ballast cleaning machines not many years ago?

The question of track renewals and other works on and around the track bed, is not so much the need for it to be done, but when and how it is done. Debates have raged in the railways for years about the advantages and disadvantages of the almost universal practice in Britain of carrying out major permanent way work at weekends. This may stem from a Victorian sentiment that Sunday travel was to be frowned upon in any case, and that those who persisted in using the railway might justifiably be penalised by having their trains delayed, or even being decanted into and out of buses for part of their sinful excursions! The detrimental commercial effects of the discomforts and late-running on Sunday journey must however in total be quite considerable.

The engineers' standard answer is that full week-end possessions are preferable to week-day partial possessions that delay business traffic, and last much longer before the work can be completed. What they do not explain is that night-time and week-end work at greatly enhanced hourly wage rates appeals to the department's staff, but involves BR in much heavier labour costs. If one points out that this concentration of major track work on Sundays does not take place on mainland Europe, the stock answer is that track occupation there is seldom as intensive as in Britain, and thus week-day engineering works are more easily carried out there. It might be interesting to find out just how the Belgians and Dutch manage their heavily used routes quite the equal of those in Britain, or the Germans to see what they do on their Rhine Valley routes, and the Swiss on the Gotthard line.

It does seem that single-line working in Britain is still too often carried out in a way apparently designed to cause the maximum delays in each direction, with trains setting back over trailing crossovers after waiting for a pilotman and travelling wrong line – that is in the reverse direction to normal – at greatly reduced speed. But modern centralised traffic control, and the widespread provision of high-speed facing crossovers alternating with trailing crossovers at reasonably close spacings, can enable traffic to keep moving reasonably well even when the engineers have full possession of one running line. More facing crossovers are needed to enable two-way working to be rapidly introduced while the other line is under engineers' possession, in a way common in mainland Europe, at reduced labour cost and without the punishing week-end delays common today. Of course, the engineers prefer to have full possession of both tracks, but how then do they renew stretches of single line of which much still exists?

Where four tracks exist 'weaving' from fast lines to slow and vice versa is now widely practised, though even here the crossovers are often unduly far apart, which reduces track capacity; priority for more crossovers is badly needed in many track renewal programmes, including of course the modest associated signalling modifications. But such facilities pay off, not merely when track work has to be undertaken but in the event of a train failing or being 'stopped for examination'. Such flexibility in operating possibilities can yield handsome dividends, on an outlay that is not great in relation to the benefits over a period of years.

Another area where civil engineers are involved is the possible raising of speed limits on curves to allow cuts in journey times, which can be done by increasing cant – that is the tilt of the track – or by allowing a higher speed than that theoretically permitted by the cant, within clearly defined rules. But the civil engineers have been slow to revise both cant and cant deficiency rules since the virtual disappearance of the unbraked, loose-coupled freight train which for so long was the alleged cause of restrictions so much more severe than those on most European railways. Speed restrictions still impose penalties on operators anxious to reduce journey times. French Railways has run for many years with confidence and no passenger discomfort round curves at speeds markedly greater than those permitted by our engineers. Admittedly both cant and cant deficiency investigations are in progress in Britain, largely in consequence of the delays in introducing the Advanced Passenger Train; but more urgency could be given for these studies.

The civil engineer's deployment of resources to deal with emergencies and with major projects is usually admirable. But his procedures for dealing with small items of maintenance often seem slow and uneconomic, perhaps because his large departmental machine is centralised and thus ill-adapted for minor tasks like mending broken windows or leaking waterpipes. Local supervisors complain, as they have done ever since railways were built, of the waste of time and money involved by the centralisation of minor maintenance in civil engineering department offices and depots. Travelling time from these centres to out-stations costs money; poor co-ordination of materials and labour supplies for small works are often the cause of delays and irritation. Employment of local building firms, known to responsible area managements, could be authorised on a more elastic scale, instead of filling in requisitions which are filed away and executed at the convenience of the engineers, rather than of the traffic department.

A distinguished civil engineer once remarked to the author that he hated small works orders; in total, he said, they often absorbed the cost of some single major new work that he would have liked to carry out, if his budget had permitted. But the cumulative effect of deferred or inadequate maintenance, even in small ways, damages the whole image of the railway. Elaborate plans for complete reconstruction of a station, 'one day, when funds permit', are no excuse for shabby paintwork, non-flushing toilets, and broken fences. Responsibility for keeping an acceptable standard ought to rest firmly with local traffic managers, and less with technical departments dominated by consideration of track, bridges and other major works.

It was bizarre, in the summer of 1984, to see men scything grass on banks beside the railway, as their ancestors had done long ago. Where else in England was this antique procedure to be found? There was justification for grass cutting in the age of steam, when a spark could ignite a grassy bank, but a general policy was laid down in 1968 that grass cutting should be discontinued; nevertheless scything and grass burning persist here and there.

The labour cost involved is far from inconsiderable. The engineers could be quicker to use plants as allies and not as enemies. London Transport long ago pioneered the stabilisation of slopes by planting suitable shrubs, etc, which also provide ground cover against seedling weeds that may constitute a nuisance through fouling the ballast. The late Pat Moran, Superintendent of the Earthworks and Gardens Section of London Transport under the Chief Civil Engineer, showed the way to reduce labour costs in weed control, and also earthworks stabilisation, by using plants intelligently. He raised countless thousands of small ground-covering shrubs from seed in his nursery, itself built out of scrap material on a piece of railway waste-land, at negligible cost. He worked on a shoestring budget; but his tiny workforce must have saved LT large sums in routine civil engineering maintenance. At the same time he provided, again at negligible cost, plants for platform flower beds, etc, to brighten stations at many suitable points on London Transport's open-air railway system – an example that BR could follow and develop with advantage.

What are the pros and cons of reducing the CE establishments and contracting out? In the early years of the railways, permanent way maintenance was sometimes entrusted for a time to the contractor who had built the railway. One would not now suggest a wholesale transfer to contractors of permanent way work because it has become intensely specialised and it also involves very close liaison with the movements department. But where a number of stations are geographically close together, group maintenance contracts covering repainting, minor structural repairs, plumbing and electrical maintenance, might be put out to competitive tender. The results obviously should be monitored by the local civil engineering inspectors and local traffic management, contracts being terminable if satisfactory service is not given. This would elminate much paperwork and travelling time. It might well prove cheaper than direct labour, and would leave the civil engineering staff freer to concentrate upon permanent way, bridges and other major repairs and new works. Naturally there would be some union opposition; but the example of many local councils that have put out work, for example, refuse collection, to contract, with savings to the ratepayers and an improved standard of service, cannot be ignored.

If the civil engineering side of BR has developed fairly steadily and progressively since nationalisation, the same can hardly be said of its mechanical and electrical engineering counterparts, who experienced the trauma of transition from steam to main line diesel and electric traction in less than a decade, with all the fundamental changes required in outlook, techniques, and training. Even before these pressures arose, life had become difficult for the former potentates of steam traction on the four great railways that were abruptly merged in British

Railways on 1 January 1948. Suddenly they became subject to a new set of standards imposed by Robin Riddles, Mechanical & Electrical Engineering Member of the Railway Executive, who quickly enforced a policy of building standard steam locomotives (based largely upon LMS design principles) with more energy but less tact than his civil engineering counterpart, J.L.C. Train, employed in the standardisation of civil engineering practices in the regions. Riddles' problems in handling men of the stature of Ivatt, Hawksworth, Peppercorn and Bulleid were only eased by some early retirements and resignations; even afterwards regional patriotism in locomotive matters remained a major if covert influence. Nor was the second period – the changeover to diesel and electric traction under the Modernisation Plan launched in 1955 after the abolition of the Railway Executive – made easier by the political interference of the Conservative Government's 1953 Transport Act, insisting upon a futile attempt to change the regions into something resembling the former railway companies. This had a quite unforeseen influence in purely technical matters. To take just one example, the 1955 Modernisation Plan rightly envisaged the elimination of the loose-coupled, hand-braked freight wagon and the universal provision of continuous brakes. After considerable discussion and study, BR technical staff at headquarters recommended standardisation of the compressed air brake, but the general managers in the regions preferred the vacuum brake. It was a case of long-term technical advantages versus adherence to established standards. The British Transport Commission accepted the regional view, a costly mistake which has had to be rectified over a long period of years. Had the decision gone the other way, the vacuum brake would have been discarded much sooner and much costly dual fitting of both types avoided. Under the Plan, as soon as funds for modernisation were available, each regional general manager and area board chairman insisted on obtaining a good slice of the cake. It would have been wiser to concentrate resources region by region, for instance by limiting the introduction at first of main line diesel traction to one, or at most two, regions, where intensive attention could be given to the changeover, with all the new maintenance facilities and staff training required. That would have been better than spreading the butter too thinly over too many pieces of bread. Meanwhile, steam should *not* have been starved of investment or management talent; as French Railways showed, the arrival of the new need not, overnight, justify neglecting the old with serious consequences to the quality of service.

The story of the transition to diesel power has been discussed by many writers. The most authoritative account, independent in its judgments but with its facts officially checked, is *British Railways Engineering, 1948–80*, by John Johnson and Robert A. Long. It explains, if it cannot justify, all the changes in policy, from the original decision to order 174 main line diesels in 14 different varieties, to be tested up to nearly two years, to the decision to speed-up the changeover. This produced acute problems for the mechanical engineers, due largely to the fact that when the 1955 Modernisation Plan was launched only seven main line diesel types existed on BR. Two had been quite unsuccessful, the 827hp North British locomotive and the ingenious Fell experimental locomotive, and five had been in only sporadic use, because of lack of interest at the highest level in the Railway Executive. Adding to the technical problems confronting the engineers was the weight given by the British Transport Commission, following political guidance, to the varying specifications proposed by the regions. After a long period of difficulty, BR today possesses a fleet of main line diesel locomotives of acceptable performance and reliability standards, though some classes have been prematurely retired.

The electrification story was not originally so complicated by political influences, the main issue being the purely technical one of the respective merits of 25kV ac or 1,500V dc traction (both of course with overhead current supply) for new electrification projects, apart from the Southern Region where, after some heartburning it was decided to ignore the technical merits of 25kV ac and to continue the extension of the 660/750V dc third rail system over the main line routes to the Kent Coast and Bournemouth.

The ac versus dc debate was only settled after considerable preliminary work had been done towards extending the existing 1500V dc Liverpool Street–Shenfield electrification over the former Great Eastern, and the London, Tilbury &

The dmu looks at home in these beautiful surroundings, but replacement is needed *(Ian S. Carr)*

A rather old-fashioned front end! *(Author)*

Forerunner of the HST that is almost forgotten; here is the Birmingham 'Blue Pullman' en route for Paddington in 1962 *(C. R. L. Coles)*
Its brilliantly successful successor looks remarkably like it *(British Rail)*

Southend lines in the London area. Perhaps at the time too much emphasis was placed upon the special advantages of 25kV for main line schemes, and the costs of the changeover were probably excessive in relation to the benefits obtained. First, the former Great Eastern lines comprise a compact, almost isolated system, with little through running to other parts of the BR network other than freight links with Thames-side. Secondly, the cost advantages of 25kV, especially in reducing the number of substations, were largely nullified by the cost of obtaining the necessary clearances of 11in between the conductor wire and bridge or tunnel structures, as then required by the Ministry of Transport. In the suburban area this involved raising many bridges, and costly works were involved in obtaining the clearances, only reduced to some extent by the adoption of a lower voltage of 6.25kV on GE and Tilbury lines (and incidentally on Glasgow suburban lines as well) in specially difficult areas. This involved the provision of special switching gear on the motor coaches or locomotives, activated by track magnets at the changeover points.

Ironically, after all this work had been carried out, experience established that lower clearances were electrically safe, and by now the whole of the 6.25kV network has been converted to 25kV!

However, the electrification of the West Coast Main Line, including Birmingham, Liverpool, and Manchester, has successfully transformed the most important single traffic artery on BR. Certainly the early designs of 25kV Bo-Bo electric locomotives in classes 81 to 85 for the London Midland electrification suffered from a number of weak points, which was perhaps surprising in view of the fairly extensive experience that had already been gained by the French Railways with 25kV ac schemes. The first important French section, on the East Region between Valenciennes and Thionville, had been brought successfully into use more than a decade before the LM electrification, and one would have thought that teething troubles on the LMR might have been reduced if French experience had been more closely studied. However, the Class 86 and Class 87 locomotives which today are the backbone of traction on Britain's only long-distance main line electrification scheme are a marked improvement on their predecessors though the riding qualities of many of the Class 86 locomotives still leave something to be desired on track not in perfect condition.

The Achilles heel of British main line coaches since nationalisation has undoubtedly been bogie design. The first post-war 'standard' designs were rather old-fashioned in interior layout but would have been quite acceptable with better riding. But the rough riding of Mark I stock at speeds over about 60mph long affected the quality of service and has not even now been quite eliminated, largely because of the failure to build any restaurant or buffet cars of the Mark II patterns, resulting in the incongruous combination of old but internally revamped Mark I buffet cars in train sets otherwise composed of vastly better modern stock.

Happily, with the arrival of Mark III stock, this anomaly is disappearing. But it remains difficult to understand how the secret of good bogie design, which produced the superbly smooth-running twelve-wheeled dining cars on the LNWR and the Midland Railway 80 years ago, and the beautiful Oerlikon electric trains of the North London and Watford lines nearly 70 years ago, seemed to have been completely lost after nationalisation, until the 1970s in fact.

Fortunately, today the Mark III stock as used both on locomotive-hauled routes and in the IC125 trains has many virtues. It rides well and quietly, and the air-conditioning provides an agreeable environment. That said, the riding on the electrified West Coast route can be lively in places where the tracks has been punished by some of the rough riding locomotives. The universal inclusion of catering facilities (even if pretty basic) is also something upon which the traveller can usually rely – a pleasant change from the often sparse provision of this facility on many Continental railways, although alas, staff problems sometimes result in short-notice withdrawal of refreshment facilities.

Three criticisms can however be made of the IC125 sets despite their many virtues. The first is the inflexibility of the trains' makeup, as compared with locomotive haulage, which leads to overcrowding at times of sudden surges in demand. The open saloon design, while modern and popular with most travellers, does not lend itself to accommodating standing passengers, except very uncomfortably indeed. However, there is nothing that can be done at short notice to add extra vehicles, though on the Eastern Region heavy passenger demand has led to some permanent strengthening of IC125 rakes. Indeed it seemed surprising that in the original formations of seven coaches two were devoted to refreshments. But a major surge of traffic really demands the running of relief trains, and in the bad old days of lower stock utilisation this could usually be done at short notice. Today, owing to enforced cost-cutting, the stock of spare sets is minimal; the fleet is fully stretched to cover the advertised timetable service.

A minor criticism has been the unpleasant smell produced when the brakes are applied, due to brake dust entering the air-conditioning system.

Lastly, although wide doors are a welcome feature for passengers with luggage, long overdue in British carriage design, why those outside door handles? It is hard to understand the persistence of BR carriage designers in providing doors with outside handles only which can be opened from within only by lowering the window – a survival from stage-coach and horse-carriage design. The drawbacks are considerable. Elderly people and those encumbered with luggage find it difficult to emerge. Once the window has been lowered, it is frequently left down whilst the train is travelling. The consequence is, of course, draughts in vehicles which, unlike Mark III, do not have air-conditioning and self-closing gangway doors. And during the heating season (which is more than half the year in Britain) open windows mean that costly electricity or diesel oil is being used to provide heat which is being blown out into the countryside for hours on end.

There is a persistent belief that outside-only door handles are a requirement of the Railway Inspectorate. But a former chief inspecting officer of railways assured the author that there was no foundation for this; he merely required that door locks could not accidentally, or too easily, be opened (as by a child) from the inside. Nothing could be more reasonable. To be fair, inside door handles were originally provided on Mark III coaches in the first batches of IC 125 units but after several cases of doors being opened at speed they were quickly removed.

Of course, sliding inside door handles of a design introduced by the former London & South Western Railway have been used for many years, but only (in theory) on stock used for commuter or short-distance journeys. These meet the safety requirements in that the pressure needed to operate them is beyond that which a small child can exert. If however the argument is that they are only safe for short distances and lower speeds, that makes nonsense of, say, the Southern Region's practice of using Class 423 4VEP stock with inside handles on, for instance, London–Portsmouth express journeys (74 miles).

Britain's insularity in this aspect of carriage design is strange. Mainland European railways have long had satisfactory inside door handles; Pullman cars in Britain had inward-opening doors. Major Rose, Chief Inspecting Officer of Railways in the UK reported that in 1983, 13 passengers died from falling out of trains and 62 were injured. 'Most of the deaths would not have occurred, or would have been unlikely, if the trains had been fitted with doors locked while the train was in motion, and with fixed windows'. While next generation Mark IV coaches will have centrally controlled doors, locked during movement, earlier Mark II and III coaches with outside handles only will still be in service for many more years yet.

There has been a certain conflict in regional managerial preferences for suburban and outer-suburban types of stock. The Southern for long appeared to cling to pre-war concepts. Compartments and slam doors with drop-light windows survive there in greater numbers than anywhere else. On the other hand, the 'Blue Trains' of the Glasgow suburban electrification scheme, when introduced in 1960, with an affinity to the 1939 LMS Liverpool area stock, set new and higher standards of amenity with excellent all-round comfort and none of the cramped 19th century appearance of the stock still then being built for the Southern.

It should be admitted that the traditional non-corridor compartment coach with six-a-side seating has two merits. It provides the greatest number of seats for any given length of train, and it also provides the greatest possible number of doors in relation to seats, which should assist rapid loading and unloading. This was the feature that appealed to the Southern Railway during its electrification schemes of the 1920s and 1930s, and it also commended itself to some elements in the

Eastern Region management – though by no means all – in the 1950s when the Southend (Victoria) line, the London, Tilbury & Southend line, and the Chingford, Enfield, Hertford and Bishops Stortford lines were being electrified.

Transplanting Southern ideas was by no means the sole influence, because of course similar philosophies originally had underlain the design of Gresley's articulated suburban train sets in pre-war steam days. Meanwhile the LNER had moved away, in planning its Liverpool Street-Shenfield electrification, to a more modern concept of open saloon stock with power-operated sliding doors, and the operating officer in charge of the Stratford District claimed that only with such a design could his timetable be observed.

It was therefore a retrograde step, hotly argued against in the Liverpool Street Planning Office, when the Eastern Region decided upon slam doors with drop-lights and, basically, a compartment type of seating. However, the disadvantages of the traditional non-corridor compartment vehicle were undeniable – liability to vandalism, inability to equalise the loading throughout the vehicle, and exposure of women to possible assault. The multiplicity of slam doors meant that a single door left open could delay the start of a train, or cause it to be stopped out of course if observed by a signalman while the train was in motion. Slam doors also are a source of danger if opened while the train is still moving in a station both by striking passengers on an adjacent platform and enabling passengers to fall out before the train has stopped.

These arguments led to an unsatisfactory compromise; a design was adopted which combined most of the drawbacks of compartment stock without its sole virtue of maximum number of seats – in essence, a combination of compartment vehicles with semi-open stock in which five-a-side seating was provided with a narrow central passage. This certainly enabled the passenger load to be equalised throughout the vehicle but it introduced a new drawback from which the conventional compartment stock had been free – the draughts which could be inflicted upon the whole of the passengers from a single drop-light left open.

This design was followed in huge numbers of vehicles, built for the Southern, and some other regions; their replacement still presents BR with a gigantic task, now in hand.

A good start was made with the new stock for the Southern's inner suburban services. The first to come was the Class 508, with open saloons and power-operated doors. The Class 508 trains have gone north to Merseyside, and the new features are incorporated in their successors, Class 455. Riding quality is generally improved and the light and airy interiors are pleasant, though, like Mark III second class coaches, there is a curious design quirk, in that the seating bays do not match the window spacing, so that some passengers sit by a solid wall, an annoying feature and one moreover that could have been avoided. It might seem just a detail, but private cars do not have passengers flanked by solid panels. The designers also seem to have departed from modern practice in the end-design of the first batch of units in Class 455, which are faintly reminiscent of trains on the Chicago Elevated of the early 1900s! The second batch has a modified front end design, which is similar to that of the Class 151 diesel multiple units, (the 'Sprinters').

Turning now to the dmu saga, the move to eliminate steam from branch secondary and lightly-used services by the substitution of diesel railcars started before the Modernisation Plan of 1955, even before the abolition of the Railway Executive in 1953, in John Elliot's time as Chairman. A so-called 'Light Weight Trains Committee' of the Executive recommended a number of pilot schemes, some of which were under way before the main line diesel plans were hatched, and the benefits were felt correspondingly sooner. The public generally welcomed the faster (70mph maximum speed) units, with their all-round windows and general airiness compared with old-fashioned steam-hauled compartment stock. Noisy the underfloor bus-type engines tended to be in the power cars, but not unacceptably so. One man at the front end, and later a conductor-guard issuing tickets on the train in place of station staff, helped to improve the economics of many branch lines whose future under steam traction must have been very doubtful indeed.

The weak feature of the policy has always been the multiplicity of designs. In principle, three or perhaps four standard BR types should have sufficed to meet the varying services operated in the Regions. In fact, the stock book today shows no fewer than 24 main classes in service, plus minor variations within classes. Most of them are on the verge of obsolescence and this presents BR with a major headache. For the replacements, contrasting ideas are still, at the time of writing, being examined. Once again the concept of the four-wheeled rail bus has been revived – the vehicle that is built to road transport standards but runs on rails. Equally, new bogie diesel-mechanical units are on trial. They are the latest in a long line of such experimental products, starting as far back as the first decade of the present century with steam and petrol railcars and gaining momentum with the Great Western Railway's AEC railcars of the 1930s. *Plus ça change!* The usual story is that, step by step, the operators and the railway mechanical engineers gradually build more strength, weight and orthodox railway practice into the design, so that it loses its original advantage of cheapness and lightness and the idea is abandoned.

However, the so-called 'Sprinter' design announced in 1984 as the replacement dmu for country branch and 'Other Provincial' services, a three-coach unit equipped with power doors, lavatories and a public address system, looked promising. One hopes that it will not follow other good designs into limbo.

The Southern, predictably, had to be different in its dieselisation of minor lines. The Hampshire stock, as it is often called, was designed to be as much like a Southern standard electric unit, such as a 2HAP (two-car units first and second class with toilets in one car), as possible, with electric traction motors and a diesel engine generating the necessary power in an above-floor driving compartment. The chief argument employed to justify demu design (instead of dmu as adopted everywhere else) was the slightly unconvincing one, that some day the secondary Hampshire lines might be electrified and then the sets, with little more than removal of the diesel engines and electric generators, would be usable as straight electric units. They have become obsolete before the lines have any prospect of being electrified.

In consequence, the attractive features of the modern dmu as used elsewhere – the all-round vision, the open saloon design – were lost. True, they had part open saloons but like the similar electric stock they had side doors of compartment style coaches, the five-a-side seats and narrow passageway. And the nominally 'main line' narrow demu sets for the Hastings line were old-fashioned in design when they were built, in 1957; today they have even lost their chief redeeming feature, the buffet cars formerly provided on certain services. Now the Tonbridge–Hastings line is being electrified these units will be replaced by electric units cascaded from other services instead of more modern designs.

Lastly, the Advanced Passenger Train. When this brainchild of the research department was introduced to the generality of railway managers, it exercised something of the same fascination that the atmospheric system had done 130 years before; it seemed an elegant and logical solution to the problem of providing very high speed without drastic remodelling of the track geometry, just as the atmospheric system had appeared to offer fast, quiet and smoke-free travel over ordinary railway tracks. Not that there weren't sceptics who distrusted the principle of putting too many new concepts – the sensor-operated tilting mechanism, the self-steering bogies, and the hydro-kinetic brake – into a single package. They were not as downright as George Hudson had been in 1846 when the Prince Consort, deeply interested all new technological developments, had asked his opinion of the atmospheric principle and the 'Railway King' had replied 'I think they're a humbug, Your Royal Highness'. And for a long time, the APT seemed to be coming along nicely; when the prototype was placed in the National Railway Museum in York and the three production series trains were authorised, its future looked reasonably assured.

The unforeseen snags that appeared on the entry into 'squadron service' were not however fundamental enough to warrant scrapping the whole project, as the atmospheric railways had been scrapped when the valve sealing the vacuum tube that provided the traction proved ineffective, quite apart from other operational disadvantages that had been ignored in the first flush of enthusiasm. On the contrary, and despite the triumph of the mechanical engineers in finding in the HST or IC125 a conventional yet highly successful alternative to the APT, it remains a long-term potential challenger to more conventional replacements in due course of both the West Coast locomotive-hauled expresses and the IC125s on the East Coast after its electrification.

So, after 35 years, BR has come up with a prize-winner – the Mark III stock both in IC125 form and as used with locomotive haulage on the London Midland and Scottish Regions; but past aberrations still have to be sorted out in replacing stock on some commuter and secondary services.

The signalling revolution — has it paid off?

Like the civil engineers, the signal engineers on BR have been spared most of the traumas that have afflicted their colleagues in the traction and rolling stock field. There are two main reasons for this. First, technological developments in outside industry have been rapid and many of them have been readily adaptable to the needs of the signal engineer. One need only mention solid-state electronics and computerisation in the field of information technology, to realise how control of train movements, in both the negative sense of ensuring safety, and the positive sense of increasing fluidity and throughput, has been facilitated by developments not primarily associated with railways at all.

In consequence, the signal engineers have been able to make out a strong case for investment in their own fields. They have been able to demonstrate very real improvements in rail safety today compared with, for example, the first decade after nationalisation. And in response to the demands for increased staff productivity, the closing of manual signalboxes over large areas and their replacement by single centralised installations has reduced the numbers of signalmen very drastically. One has only to recall that formerly a small one-man box, staffed on a three-shift basis, would have required a permanent establishment of probably five posts to cover rest-day and holiday period working, to appreciate the scope for savings in this direction. It must however also be remembered that the reduction in signalmen was to some extent counterbalanced by the increase in the number of signal technicians, the 'linemen' and 'signal fitters' of an earlier age.

The numbers of signal boxes closed under some of these centralisation schemes are impressive:

New centralised signalboxes	*No of signalboxes replaced*
Kings Cross	57
Doncaster	61
Saltley	49
Preston	87
Motherwell	68

But the policy does impose some drawbacks. Signalmen no longer observe trains directly, which can be disadvantageous in an emergency, for example when there is an open door, requiring the train to be stopped for examination. And a local industrial dispute, where just one or two signalmen walk off the job or have to be sent home, can paralyse a major section of the railway (as was the case once in the Warrington box), whereas a smaller manual box could be worked by staff not involved in the dispute, or be simply switched out.

It is interesting to compare the signalling conditions under which today's Inter-City trains operate with those of 30 or 40 years ago. It is still the case that information and instructions to train drivers are conveyed intermittently, by fixed signals; but how much more effectively! The great enemy used to be fog. A real 'pea-souper' could reduce visibility to such a point that drivers would have to creep from signal to signal, relying more upon sounds from the track than anything else to establish their locality and awaiting the explosion of detonators to confirm signal siting. Semaphore signals, usually oil-lit, often had (some still have) the arms at the top of a tall post to be seen above bridges or buildings. In thick fog the arm and its lamp were lost in the mist and on occasions, halted at a signal, firemen have had to climb the signal ladder to ascertain whether the signal was 'on' or 'off'.

This lies mostly long in the past. Today's drivers run confidently in foggy weather, aided by strongly visible colour-light signal aspects virtually at eye level and the audible cab-signalling of the standard BR automatic warning system (aws). It must also be added that the thick yellow 'smog' of earlier days is now almost extinct, following the Clean Air legislation and the virtual disappearance of house heating and cooking through the burning of raw coal. We may discharge subtler poisons into the atmosphere, from cars and from industrial plants but the products of coal combustion no longer combine with atmospheric moisture to produce the famous 'London particulars' associated with Victorian melodrama.

However, the path has not always led upwards to ever sunnier pastures. In the first years after nationalisation a great debate raged over the introduction of what was then termed automatic train control. The British Transport Commission wanted it to be introduced universally, but was frightened by the cost, and also by some criticism of the only system then widely in use, the Great Western's electro-mechanical ramp-and-shoe. This was crude by modern standards but generally effective; the Strowger-Hudd electro-magnetic alternative, in use on a small scale on the London, Tilbury & Southend section of the LMS, seemed more promising but had not been tested and approved on a large scale.

On top of this debate, there was a school of thought – largely in the Southern Region – which argued that, pound for pound, greater additional safety, as well as improved operating efficiency, could be obtained through investing in colour-light signalling and continuous track circuiting than by supplementing visual with audible signal indications.

In the event, the standardisation of colour-light signalling and installation of aws proceeded more or less hand in hand; we cannot tell whether extending the former at the expense of the latter, within the limits of overall investments constraints, would have yielded greater benefits. One sometimes wonders whether the installation of aws on some secondary lines with moderate speeds and infrequent services is really justified. Certainly the Southern's electric network as a whole runs so well in intensively-signalled areas that drivers are often receiving 'warning' buzzes from a long series of double-yellow indications from a train ahead, without markedly having to reduce speed. Yet the dreadful disaster at Harrow & Wealdstone on 8 October 1952, 11 miles from Euston on the West Coast Main Line which would have been averted or greatly mitigated by aws cannot be forgotten.

While the mainstream of signalling development has therefore been pretty constant, there has been an undercurrent of dissatisfaction with the perpetuation of the long-established principle of intermittent indications to drivers, and a desire to move towards continuous instructions regarding the correct and safe speed to maintain. For a long time after the creation of the Derby Technical Centre with its substantial funding of research, much effort went into the search for a more advanced signalling system. But it did not lead in a direction really compatible with the existing transition from 'stick and string' – manually operated semaphores – to colour-light signalling. It must be remembered that, except on the Southern Railway, the commonest form of colour-light signals, in their early days of the 1920s and 1930s had been on an individual basis, replacing isolated semaphore distant signals here and there. The Great Western, always declining to follow other railways' practices, introduced a curious type of 'colour-light' which simply replaced previous semaphore arms with electric signal lights visible in daylight. In contrast the Southern, pioneering four-aspect colour lights on the Holborn Viaduct – Elephant and Castle section as early as 1926, made the changeovers pretty well complete as regards running lines, only sidings, etc, being left with manually-operated semaphores or ground discs.

The 'new look' at Derby in the 1960s, however, was not directed towards spot replacement of existing signals or indeed anything compatible with traditional block system-cum-semaphore working. It was to provide continuous contact between control centres and train drivers, with full control of speeds as well as conveying information. The first move was the development of the so-called 'wiggly-wire'; it comprised coils mounted below the train and two insulated wires continuously laid between the rails, providing (by induction) continuous signal aspect and other communications to the driver. The second was SRAWS, or 'Signal Repeating Automatic Warning System', which provided a colour-light signal indication in the driver's cab showing the aspect of the signal just passed until within 275 yards of the signal ahead, when a change to the indication of that signal was made. Both these systems were given quite extensive trials but were abandoned in view of cost and the rather limited extra advantages they offered.

A more practical and cost-effective system has been the control system installed primarily for the benefit of the Advanced Passenger Trains at speeds in excess of 125mph on the Euston – Glasgow route. It provides track-mounted 'transponders'; at each one an inducted signal from the train to the transponder bounces back with fixed information and passed via the train-borne microprocessor indicates to the driver his maximum permitted speed beyond that transponder.

It is a fact of history that major improvements in the technology of railway safety are often linked with some serious accident. The Harrow & Wealdstone disaster of October 1952 did not lead to the design of aws but it certainly accelerated its introduction on BR main lines. The unprecedented Moorgate accident on London Transport, when a train on the Northern City Line collided at speed with the tunnel dead-end wall beyond the platform led to a fundamental re-think about the control of train speed when approaching a terminus. One reform was the institution of 'Moorgate control' under which on certain terminal lines, particularly on underground routes, the signal governing entry to the platform does not clear, and on London Transport and the few BR routes fitted with trip arm apparatus the train stop trip is not cleared, if a train's speed exceeds a prescribed figure during its approach. Moreover its subsequent speed is monitored until it correctly halts. The second and very simple reform has been to eliminate the green aspect at the entry to a dead-end terminal track and to show instead a single yellow aspect, now standard at all terminal tracks where colour-light signals are used, and such an obvious improvement that one wonders why it was not adopted from the outset.

A rather similar situation has arisen from the Morpeth derailment in 1984. Here though there was some previous history. In 1969 the northbound Aberdonian sleeping car train overturned and six passengers were killed when the Morpeth curve was entered at a speed of 82mph (admitted by the driver at the accident enquiry) whereas the line speed at this point was 40mph. After the enquiry the Ministry of Transport Inspecting Officer of Railways recommended the installation of a fixed advance warning board at braking distance and a permanent magnet aws giving an audible cab signal as when passing a signal at caution. But it was a pity that this simple and relatively cheap expedient was not made a requirement for all permanent speed restrictions, especially in view of the subsequent increase in train speeds. Instead a complex set of guidelines was laid down by the Ministry, requiring this measure to be introduced only at places where the line speed is 75mph or more and the restriction is to less than two-thirds of the line speed.

There have been subsequent cases of derailment which probably would have been averted if the aws audible warning had been given, even though it is still within a driver's power to cancel the warning and thus avoid a brake application should he fail to realise exactly where he is. In 1984 the second Morpeth derailment was fortunately unattended by loss of life, but most likely would not have taken place at all had an audible warning magnet been in place. Curiously, because the line speed is reduced in stages approaching Morpeth, the lesser speeds did not come within the Ministry guidelines for installing permanent speed indicators and aws magnets. There seems a strong case for reviewing the guidelines, especially as the cost of extending the aws warning would not be great.

BR has halted, with some uncertainty, on the threshold of the 'very high speed' age. There is a barrier, something akin to air transport's sound barrier, that seems to exist in signalling techniques once speeds rise substantially in excess of 125mph or thereabouts. Four-aspect colour light signalling, coupled with aws, has coped quite successfully with the introduction of the IC125 trains, but the confident prediction of 155mph by the Advanced Passenger Train has been noticeably muted. Even the new APT brand-name IC225, representing the metric equivalent of 140mph, suggests that the official view of top speeds has been toned down a little. The lack of a signalling system tailor-made for the higher speeds, more sophisticated than fixed-location transponders, capable of installation at reasonable cost over very long distances and also applicable to other forms of traction and rolling stock using the same routes, may well have been a factor. Moving into the realm of very high speed involves a great deal more than just building trains; it requires a re-think of the whole philosophy of operation, signalling and telecommunications. The APT concept was perhaps adopted too enthusiastically without enough consideration of all its implications. The assumption of compatibility with existing rail technology, apart from obvious questions of signal sighting and pathing of slower-moving traffic, was made rather too easily. The French, in their logical and thoroughgoing way, eschewed compromise and moved into the era of very high speed via TGV, which is not just a train but a new system of rail technology, largely isolated from the conventional network, not as completely as Japan did with its Shinkansen high-speed network, but still effectively. By comparison, in Britain we seem to have hedged. Even at 140mph APT or IC225 will need something more than the standard four-aspect signalling can give and one suggestion is an extra warning by transponder indication on the driver's control desk, related to caution indications from visual signals ahead.

Nevertheless, to be practical, is not 125mph adequate to give acceptable journey times over the relatively short distances of most of our important express trains? Is the time-saving, as between maxima of 125mph and 140mph or 155mph, really worthwhile in commercial terms?

This leads into another important question, namely the ever-increasing capital costs of more sophisticated signal systems. Accepting the advantages in safety and operational efficiency from multiple-aspect colour-light signalling combined with fairly simple but reasonably effective BR standard aws, do not the huge new centralised boxes such as Victoria, with all their theoretical advantages, swallow up too much of BR's limited investment allocation? They may be an operator's paradise and a signal engineer's dream come true, but how much annual saving do they produce in labour costs (in hard cash, not just disestablishment of posts) and how much improvement directly perceptible to the passenger, in terms of train speeds, frequency and punctuality?

Some considerable experience of assessing proposals for new works has led this author to take a slightly sceptical view of the way in which the understandable enthusiasm of technical departmental chiefs can take hold. Sir John Elliot recalls a story of the great Raoul Dautry, who when Chief Engineer of the Nord Railway presented a massive investment plan to the Board presided over by Baron Rothschild. At the end of the presentation, very ably made, Baron Rothschild remarked: 'Gentlemen, there are three ways of ruining oneself. The first is through women; it is the most enjoyable. The second is with racehorses; it is the most exciting. The third is with engineers' ideas; it is the most certain'.

It has perhaps too long been accepted that electrification schemes must involve remodelling the railway – signalling completely modernised, track strengthened with continuous welded rail (if that does not already exist), stations rebuilt or improved, and so on. The total outlay may well kill the financial attraction of the scheme. It is a philosophy contrary to that of the great electrifier, Sir Herbert Walker of the Southern, who insisted that, beyond providing electricity supply and traction units, other improvements must be separately justified. He got a great mileage of the Southern electrified on this basis from a hard-headed board of directors, quite as tough as the Treasury is today, even though it sometimes meant electric trains using stations still lit by gas lamps!

At the other end of the spectrum, the London Midland's main line electrification involved building virtually a new railway, with the complete reconstruction of Euston, Birmingham New Street, Coventry and so on. Probably that was justified because the LMS had such a backlog of overdue modernisation. But elsewhere the automatic assumption of comprehensive modernisation has been perhaps too easily accepted. One recalls a signal sighting inspection on the Colchester–Clacton–Walton line before its electrification, at which all were convinced that, with a certain amount of re-siting, the existing semaphore signalling could well remain and be compatible with the installation of overhead electric power supply to the trains. There may well be other cases where, if the signal engineer can be persuaded to 'pipe down', the overhead can be strung up much more cheaply.

It can reasonably be suggested that the signal engineers have had a good innings. Helped along by the astonishing advances in the field of information technology, they have achieved a lot. Indeed it can be said that with the modern signalling of today, with the equipment functioning as it was designed to do, signalmen's errors have been virtually eliminated. That is good as far as it goes. But signalling investment has gone far beyond that stage, with centralised control and sophistication, yet (importantly) leaving one major weak link in the safety chain – the driver. As we have seen, drivers can and still very occasionally do make mistakes, running past signals at danger. Where is the automation that will completely eliminate their errors? Harrow set the ball rolling right across BR with aws, building on the Great Western's pioneering 'automatic train control'; but 30 years later (and nearly 80 years since the first GWR experiments) it is fitted on only just over half of BR's track. Even then it is not foolproof since there have been a number of accidents over the years where drivers have acknowledged an aws warning and still run by danger signals. Another accident in 1984 (at Wembley) showed that despite aws, the potential for disaster still exists, given the right combination of circumstances, although fortunately on the evening of the Wembley accident the fates were kind.

Higher speeds leave less room for errors of judgement or carelessness and some of the signalling investment should have gone towards more positive elimination of driver error. The technology exists; it needs the will, and above all the cash. If BR firms up its thinking about high speed for the future, renouncing the extra few miles an hour but extending the 125mph network into some hitherto neglected areas, the thirst of the signalling men for huge dollops of investment may have to be curbed; a period of consolidation rather than spectacular advances is what the railways may need most of all.

4

Fair Fares

A common experience of many airline passengers is that of sitting next to a fellow-traveller with whom one enters into conversation, and discovering that two very different fares have been paid for the identical journey. It leads to feelings of frustration and annoyance, because only the experienced or well-informed are usually able to select the most advantageous fare from a whole range of options usually referred to as the 'airline jungle'. There are bargains to be snapped up at the so-called 'bucket shops', but this can be risky unless one is knowledgeable. Again, fares per kilometre flown seem to vary quite capriciously; London to Düsseldorf may cost five, six or seven times as much per kilometre as London to Los Angeles.

Until fairly recently, rail travel was on the whole free from this complexity. British fares were not quite as closely distance-related as on the Continent, where, if one knew the kilometrage to one's destination, the cost of the ticket could often be calculated with accuracy. But in general the principle of so much per mile, varied only by different scales of comfort, held good on BR. Fares were free from the enormous complexity of rail freight rates which had so long been controlled by statutory provisions with different classes for different commodities and literally millions of individual rates in force.

Obviously passenger traffic has to be charged on the basis of published tariffs. The idea of each passenger striking a bargain at the booking office is laughable – though it has been known to happen in some airports when a flight has been about to leave with empty seats! British railways have always worked on the basis of scales originally laid down as maxima in each company's Act of Parliament. First class, in the early days, was seen as equivalent to the 'inside' of the stage coaches; second

class, the 'outside'; and third class (until Gladstone's Cheap
Trains Act of 1844) was for those who could not have afforded
the stage coach at all and would either have walked or ridden in
a carrier's cart.

The rise of the third class (nowadays second) to become the
dominant sector of the market is a long and sometimes
diverting matter of history, from the very early days when a
railway chairman agreed to provide third class accommodation
(of a sort) in wagons on the very early morning goods trains,
since this would 'not merely provide the industrious poor with
an opportunity for travel but also encouragement for early
rising'.

The notion that fair fares involve an equivalent charge for
every mile travelled is a deep-rooted one; it seems to conform to
natural justice, to pay twice as much to travel from London to
Edinburgh (393 miles) as from London to Bradford (195
miles). And, by and large, once some of the early extravagances
of competitive fare-cutting had been eliminated towards the
latter part of the 19th century, this principle prevailed
generally, the only significant variation being an element of
'taper' on long journeys.

Between the wars, a very simple fare structure of $1\frac{1}{2}$d
(0.625p) per mile, third class, and $2\frac{1}{2}$d (1.041p) first class, for
single journeys existed, small percentage adjustments upwards
being permitted in 1937. In fact, however, the great majority of
journeys were out-and-return, and for these, single fare plus a
third was charged in the form of the 'monthly return' ticket.
Thus, most passengers paid 1d (0.42p) per mile out-and-back
third class for ordinary journeys. Day return tickets (nowadays
called 'Awayday') were issued at about single fare, sometimes
rounded up, and in addition there were day excursions and
half-day excursions at specially low fares, justified on a costing
basis by the full loading of the trains on which they were
available and also, often, by the opportunity of using at
week-ends train sets that otherwise would have run on
Mondays to Fridays only.

This principle of standard charges had two merits. First, it
was intelligible to everyone, and second, it seemed to appeal to
logic. But obviously any simple, rigid tariff has disadvantages.
Some people, who would like to travel, and who could in fact be

carried at marginal or negligible cost because spare capacity exists, may find the price too high, while others, such as business men on expense accounts, might be prepared to pay more if the service is convenient for them; in economic jargon, the demand price schedules of different types of customer show wide variations.

Attempts to match these variations by differential pricing bring an obvious problem. Those prepared to pay the higher price may find ways of travelling at the cheaper scale. There are various techniques for preventing this, the most obvious being the limitation of 'Awayday' ticket availability to periods after the morning commuter peak hour, it being assumed that commuter demand is relatively inelastic. Excursion trips before the second world war used to pose another question; how did one stop the ordinary traveller from making his journey at this specially cheap price? (The half-day excursion fare was sometimes much less than the ordinary single fare.) The method adopted was to prohibit passengers from taking luggage with them on excursion trains; but it was sometimes hard to enforce: was a large shopping bag luggage or was it not?

At various times other expedients have been tried. A hilarious example occurred many years ago on the former Lancashire & Yorkshire Railway which advertised cheap day excursions from Oldham to Blackpool at a fare of 1s (5p) for ladies and 1s 6d (7½p) for men, an interesting assessment of demand elasticity. A zealous local official was tipped off (perhaps as a hoax) that a lot of the lady purchasers of the 1s tickets would actually be men in drag! He then attempted personally to satisfy himself of the sex of each passenger passing the barrier, which held up the crowd until the robust Lancastrians lost their patience, charged the barrier and knocked the officious gentleman flat and unconscious.

'Market pricing', which means differential charging for identical or virtually identical services, emerged on BR after its fares ceased to be regulated by charges schemes that had to be approved by the Transport Tribunal set up under the 1947 Transport Act. BR is no longer a monopoly needing regulation but is competing hard, sometimes desperately, against alternative services by coach, airline and (above all) the private car.

Once charges schemes disappeared, BR began to examine the market with the object of simultaneously maximising receipts and also, if possible, passenger journeys. (The two objectives are occasionally in conflict.) Trial and error has been the guiding principle, and this sometimes leads to accusations of inconsistency or over-frequent change. But BR today depends more on its passenger receipts than its freight, and can at least be thankful that it is now free from Government intervention over fares increases which had had a disastrous effect in the early 1950s, the classic case being Winston Churchill's instruction to the then Minister of Transport to issue a Direction halting an increase in passenger fares approved by the Transport Tribunal.

Passenger fares, having at last ceased to be legally authorised tariffs, are now, so far as practicable, fixed according to the time-honoured maxim that used to govern freight rates, namely 'charging what the traffic will bear'. Its advocates of course argue, as they used to do in the case of freight rates that the maxim is better expressed as '*not* charging what the traffic will *not* bear'.

How in practice did BR apply this principle? A relatively high base or standard fare was fixed, not necessarily closely related to the distance between any pair of points, though obviously this is the major influence. Thereafter a wide range of discounts was offered, subject to various limitations or conditions designed to preserve the full fare receipts from those passengers able to pay it.

In the summer of 1984 the following types of fare were on offer (apart from special local fares in particular areas), making no less than 15 in all:

Standard single	Family Railcard
Standard return	Senior Citizen's Railcard
Week-end return	Young Person's Railcard
Season tickets	Disabled Person's Railcard
'Inter-City savers'	Journey Club Railcard
'Awayday return'	'Sea–Rail Special' tickets
'Railriders Club'	Passenger Promotion 'free' tickets
'Nightrider'	

In addition, supplements were chargeable for sleeping cars, seat reservations, and the sole surviving Pullman train on the

Euston–Manchester route. Moreover the standard single and return, and one or two of the discount tickets were available for first class as well as second class.

Except for the first few types of ticket, either proof of entitlement was required or there were limitations on the use of the ticket, usually by day of the week or time of day. Compared with the simplicity of the former nation-wide standard tariffs, this range of options could be described as a 'jungle' – a term which used to be applied to the much more complex area of freight charging. BR eventually decided that market pricing, however attractive in theory, had over-reached itself, and that simplification was overdue; in September 1984 a new 'saver' discount wrapping up a number of existing concessions was announced, to come into force in the following year. This was a welcome reform.

The practical disadvantages of multiple fare scales are obvious. First of all, potential rail passengers may not have the time or the inclination to puzzle out just what is the most advantageous fare available to them. (It may be argued that this also applies to air travel, but in that case, usually much larger sums of money are at stake.) Secondly, it is difficult to ensure that railway staff are informed about all the options available and are completely up-to-date in their knowledge. Nothing exasperates a would-be passenger more than to encounter a travelling ticket collector who professes ignorance of some travel concession that has been advertised. Of course, it is understandable that a booking clerk dealing with a queue of impatient travellers may have failed to study the latest circular or have no time to explain it to an enquirer; to be a high-speed ticket-seller and simultaneously a travel consultant to a flustered elderly lady may be expecting too much.

Much turns upon the publicity given to the various fare options involved in market pricing. Advertising by television spots is so quick that it is difficult to get across an adequately specific message that will remain in the viewer's memory. So it was a welcome move when in October 1983 BR got round to printing a comprehensive guide to purchasing a rail ticket, describing with examples the fare options then available. But one comment must be made. The 1983 booklet was publicised as being 'available' at stations and ticket agencies. Now people calling at such places are mostly already motivated to travel by rail. Surely the prime need is to bring the various options and opportunities to the notice of those people who are *not* proposing to use the train, the millions who automatically use their cars (or possibly National Express coaches) and who never enter a railway station or ask a travel agent about rail fares and services. To break through the barrier of indifference, prejudice or ignorance perhaps area managers should arrange through their staffs to make contact with leading newsagents in each main town or village in their area and arrange for a copy of such a booklet to be delivered with the newspaper at every address served. Such delivery of advertising matter through newsagents is now widespread.

There is also a problem of reaching the top end of the market, which is not so price-conscious but very quality-conscious. Here BR's Executive fare offering subsidiary services in an inclusive total is only likely to attract business on a few routes, but it is certainly a very worthwhile experiment. The same can hardly be said of the decision to withdraw all first class 'Awayday fares, which was strongly condemned by the Central Transport Consultative Committee. It was based on the belief that first class travellers outside the peak period are well-heeled and would swallow the extra cost of an ordinary return ticket. This appears to have been mistaken; on an important Southern Region commuter route where the second class Awayday was £4 and the first class £6, the effective result of the change was to double the cost of the latter to £12, with the result that regular day travellers who had previously enjoyed first class comfort either changed to using their cars, or went second class. This was confirmed in conversation with experienced travelling ticket collectors and station staff in the Southern Region.

After all the variations that have been played on the theme of market pricing, perhaps the main point that emerges is the need for any fare structure to be attractive to those who do *not* now travel by rail, even more than to the captive market. Is enough done to drag the motorist planning a journey away from his road maps and towards the BR timetable?

5

Inter-City, Quality Service, and the Problem Region

'Inter-City' as a marketing ploy must be adjudged a great success. Germany has paid BR the compliment of copying it for both rail and internal airline services and Switzerland for rail services, both countries rendering it in English. It is easily remembered as a brand name. But when one comes to study it closely, it appears to cover at least three distinct concepts within BR.

First, there is the Inter-City poster map showing in simplified diagrammatic form the principal main line passenger routes, and the journey times from London by the fastest trains. Next, there is the timetable symbol 125 offering the image of a particular type of train providing a specific quality of service. Lastly comes the concept of Inter-City as a self-contained business within BR, under its own Sector Director and producing its own financial results.

None of these aspects is clear-cut and self-contained. For instance, the Inter-City map includes services which are not within the province of the Sector Director (Inter-City) but of the Sector Director (London & South East). On service quality, moreover, how can one classify as Inter-City such SR trains as those which lack all catering services (London–Folkestone–Dover) or which stop at intervals of, successively, 24 miles, 6 miles, 12 miles, 12 miles, 11 miles, 9 miles (Waterloo–Portsmouth)? Surely the only genuine Inter-City types of service are those provided by the IC125 high-speed trains and the London Midland/Scottish Region electrified expresses? They offer a standard worthy of the brand name, which is devalued when it is applied to, for instance, a

Waterloo–Portsmouth train, heavily loaded, with standing commuters, achieving an overall average speed of 46mph with seven stops in a journey of no more than 74 miles. Perhaps the Waterloo–Southampton–Bournemouth fast services just scrape into the Inter-City category, though the stock is old-fashioned by standards elsewhere and riding quality is not good. But to show an Inter-City map with virtually nothing in the South of England (where living standards are highest) would certainly look odd. The answer may be for the Southern Region to provide some trains that are really worthy of the accolade, instead of just the extended commuter services that prevail today.

Another apparent oddity is the omission from Inter-City services of pairs of major cities, such as Liverpool and Manchester, or Edinburgh and Glasgow; their train services are classed as 'Provincial' rather than Inter-City.

The Inter-City 'business' is set out in the BR Corporate Plan for 1983–88 with estimated financial results as though it were a subsidiary company owing its own assets and employing its own staff. But it is not really a 'business' but a series of operations within the passenger business of BR. The forecast results in the Plan were:

Losses in £ millions

1983	159
1984	121
1985	105
1986	78
1987	72
1988	66
1989	–

The target set by the Government, according to the Plan, has been 'to make steady progress towards a five per cent return on assets after charging depreciation at current cost'.

During one of the periodical re-appraisals of BR's position, efficiency and prospects demanded by government in the 1960s, a firm of consultants insisted that BR was composed of a number of separate businesses, each of which needed to be separately managed. There may well have been justification for this in regard to the so-called ancillary activities, and for establishing a supplier-and-customer relationship with, for instance, British Rail workshops, now BREL. But when it was applied to train services, the concept became artificial. Neither the revenues nor the expenses could be accurately separated and it became necessary to invent theoretical principles upon which huge chunks of expenditure could be allocated on more of a statistical than an accounting (ie business) basis. Ironically, perhaps, the former Railway Clearing House, had it survived, *might* have been able to produce financial accounts for the 'businesses' – though at a huge cost in manpower and in computer time.

Simply calling a train 'Inter-City' produces nothing in real terms other than a marketing brand name. As regards revenues and costs within the complex of services provided and costs incurred by BR, unremitting attention certainly needs to be given to adjusting, increasing, reducing or improving individual services in all Sectors, on both a short- and a long-term revenue basis. But the highly notional 'results' of Sector businesses do not of themselves do anything to promote a more efficient railway. Inter-City, Freight, Parcels, London & SE as well as other Provincial Services overlap in their use of the infrastructure and in some cases in the use of traction and rolling stock. For instance, locomotives used for passenger trains by day may be assigned to the Freight Sector by night. An even more artificial concept is that of 'prime user' whereby if, say, 'Inter-City' is considered to be the chief user of a section of track, that 'business' is charged with all the infrastructure costs arising from it, apart from the 'avoidable costs' which would be saved if other users, for instance the Freight or the PTE Sectors were to cease using it. Application of this highly theoretical economic notion can produce curious and anomalous results in practice.

Clearly, however, there is merit in having Sector Directors for (a) marketing a particular group of rail services and (b) continous monitoring of the quality of those services. They can have a customer-and-supplier relationship with the Regions which actually provide services. They can be in a position of prescribing standards, provided these are realistic; but can they be *really* in command of resources themselves, in a way that can make them accountable for the financial results?

The concept of Sectors and Sector financial results appeals to Government because it seems to rationalise the way in which the funding of BR is carried out. Its artificiality does not worry civil servants or Ministers. Perhaps this rather elaborate and artificial concept could be simplified. The level of Government funding should be subject to BR providing overall a satisfactory level of train services, which could be assessed by some impartial body such as the pre-war Railway Rates Tribunal or the post-war Transport Tribunal reporting upon the financial support required for the services to be maintained in satisfactory quantity and quality – an efficiency audit, in fact. In the case of Inter-City, one could expect a definition of service quality to embrace speed, comfort, reasonably infrequent stops, reservation of seats and adequate refreshment facilities. As in Germany, Inter-City trains should be so designated in the timetable (and carry better destination boards than the present paper stickers). 'Inter-City' badges, if not a distinctive uniform, should be issued to train staff in contact with passengers. Lastly, an Inter-City Inspectorate should be established, separate from the Regional organisations, to monitor service quality on behalf of the Sector Director, much as the former East Coast Inspectors did in pre-war days on the LNER.

The concept of superior service has been due for restoration since the almost complete disappearance of Pullman and named prestige trains during the 1970s, when a kind of austerity phase seemed to settle in. The survival of a few names in the timetable attached to otherwise standard HST or London Midland electric trains is not very convincing. Accordingly, the introduction of 'Executive Service' in 1984, available on some 65 trains, was a well justified experiment. It offered first class passengers a reserved seat, a promise of meal service at the seat and a voucher for the cost of meals, together with car-hire facilities at destination if required. Whether patronage will be sufficient can only be decided after a lengthy trial. Moreover 'Executive' facilities must be reliably provided and not withdrawn at a moment's notice as had happened on one or two occasions.

The introduction of a train telephone service – something that has been available in several other countries for some time

– is another fringe benefit upon which judgment must be deferred. Some businessmen have alleged that they travel by train just because it gives them peace for a time from the telephone! One remembers the trial typewriting and dictation facilities offered on the short-lived City to City expresses between London (Broad Street) and Birmingham (New Street) before the first world war, or the hairdressing saloon on the Flying Scotsman of 1928. History has a way of repeating itself; the experimental train video film service which BR has tried out merely repeats the LNER's cinema coach of the inter-war years.

One concept of superior service is that if it is to support a general public view of BR as highly efficient, it should not rely upon gimmicks but diffuse the benefits to second class as well as first, and aim at reproducing the consistent and reliable standards that were formerly experienced by passengers using the chief named trains, or the all-Pullman trains, on several Regions of BR. The letter 'C' seems to cover most of the constituents – catering, cleanliness, courtesy and celerity!

There is a problem facing BR's attempt to establish a standard, recognisable image of Inter-City as a nation-wide transport service; it is the markedly different character of the Southern compared with the other Regions. The image of BR in the minds of many members of what may be considered the Establishment – politicians, senior civil servants, merchant bankers, stockbrokers, company directors and newspaper editors – often tends to be formed by daily commuter experience of the Southern Region, which serves the favoured residential areas of Hampshire, Surrey, Sussex and Kent. Every morning the executive brief-cases stream into London from Sunningdale and Guildford, Haywards Heath and Brighton, Tunbridge Wells and East Grinstead. Many reach the City via that antiquated but on the whole effective person-mover known as the 'Drain' from Waterloo, BR's Waterloo & City underground line. Others walk over London Bridge, while from Charing Cross and Victoria the seats of power in Westminster and Whitehall and the board rooms of St James's Square are nearby.

Yet these passengers, who would certainly smile at being described as a 'small and often privileged minority'* when they

* See page 174

travel on the crowded Southern commuter trains, fly to Aberdeen or Glasgow on business, or are driven in company cars down the motorways to their appointments in Cardiff or Birmingham. So they see too little of the high quality service that BR provides on major Inter-City routes and tend to judge the railways by what in recent times has become BR's problem Region.

The Southern has always been 'different'; the former Southern Railway prided itself on this. Under the leadership of Sir Herbert Walker it improved out of all knowledge after the grouping of 1923, with clean, punctual and quite fast electric services, and steam-hauled expresses with considerable prestige value. The Atlantic Coast Express, the Continental Boat trains, the Bournemouth Belle and the Ocean Liner specials could face comparison with the best the other companies could offer apart from the few and short-lived streamliners of the LNER and the LMS. Southern stations had largely been modernised or, at least, cleaned up and face-lifted. Excellent train catering services were provided by the Pullman Car Company or Frederick Hotels on practically all the principal trains. Even secondary main lines such as Waterloo – Portsmouth and Charing Cross – Hastings were well served.

The popularity of the improved Southern Railway at the end of the Walker regime even caused some jealousy among the larger companies, which were inclined sometimes to describe the Southern as merely a 'tramway'. Sir Ronald Matthews, Chairman of the LNER, once snorted 'The Southern have no problems' – in reply to which it was suggested that if indeed this was so, it was because they seemed to have solved them. And despite obtaining 75 per cent of its revenue from passengers, which traditionally was supposed to be a less profitable business than freight, the Southern paid better dividends on its equity stock than the LNER which earned over 60 per cent of its revenue from freight. Today things are still different, but in rather another sense.

One rather cynical observer commented that 'nowadays the Southern does not run on electricity or diesel oil but on momentum'. Allowing for a little picturesque exaggeration, the point is valid that the management style imposed by Walker in the 1920s and 1930s has been slowly running down. The

Southern has no high-speed trains, for instance, running at 100mph let alone any at 125mph, and no catering on a whole group of so-called Inter-City services including all the Kent Coast and Continental trains. At the cathedral and university city of Guildford, one of the Southern's prime commuting centres, the railway station has for many years been dilapidated, almost ruinous, to an extent that would not have been tolerated by the former Southern Railway management.

Since the end of the second world war the Southern has admittedly introduced some improvements in journey speeds, and even more in service frequency, though speeds are seldom comparable with those on other Regions of BR. The chief improvements both in journey times and frequency, have come on those lines electrified in the 1960s, between London, Southampton and Bournemouth, and between London, Folkestone and Dover. (Unfortunately one cannot include the services over the former London, Chatham & Dover main line to the North Kent Coast among the beneficiaries.) On the Bournemouth service, one may consider that, despite improved speed and frequency, quality has declined so far as riding comfort and catering standards are concerned. On the old South Eastern lines, improvements in speed and frequency are offset by the total loss of catering services, as well as by rough riding compared with the old steam stock. Elsewhere on the Southern, especially on the Central Section, standards have scarcely improved since electrification in the 1930s. So far as the quickest times in 1939 and 1984 are concerned, gains and losses appear as follows:

	Fastest times	
	(weekdays M-F)	
	1939 hr. m.	*1983* hr. m.
Waterloo–Bournemouth	1.56*	1.38
Waterloo–Salisbury	1.21*	1.24†
Waterloo–Portsmouth & Southsea	1.30	1.26
Waterloo–Exeter	3.12*	3.16†
Victoria–Brighton	1.00	0.53
Victoria–Bognor	1.34	1.39
Victoria–Eastbourne	1.23	1.27
Victoria–Hastings	1.35	1.58

Charing Cross–Dover (Priory)	1.34*	1.17
Charing Cross–Hastings	1.35*	1.35
Victoria–Margate	1.30*	1.35

* Steam
† diesel, remainder electric in 1983
The Exeter times are not directly comparable since those of 1939 are for the Atlantic Coast Express, and for 1983 the services calling at most intermediate stations between Salisbury and Exeter.

The brightest jewel in the Southern's crown used to be Brighton, with the standard departures 'on the hour' all with Pullman cars and including the much-loved Brighton Belle. There were no fewer than 18 Pullman services in 1939, all non-stop. Today, Brighton has no non-stops and many departures are at odd times. There are 13 buffet car workings, but none after 21.32; gone are the 22.00, 23.00 and 24.00 with Pullmans, beloved of Brighton commuters after an evening in London.

Some other comparisons can be made with Southern Railway services before the second world war. Salisbury (population 36,000, 84 miles from London) is an interesting case. In 1939 there were six expresses from Waterloo, all with full restaurant car service, two of them non-stop, the fastest time 81 minutes, and also 12 stopping services without catering. In 1984 there were six semi-fast trains, five of which had catering, though only a 'micro-buffet', with a standard pattern of three intermediate stops, fastest time 84 minutes; in addition there were nine stopping trains (one with a micro-buffet).

Hastings & St Leonards (75,000 inhabitants, and 63 miles from London) is another case. By the South Eastern route from Charing Cross, Cannon Street or London Bridge, in 1939 with steam traction there were nine trains, six of which had Pullman cars, with a varied pattern of stops, the best time being 95 minutes. In 1984 there were 18 diesel-electric trains with either 17 or 15 intermediate stops, and no catering facilities. From Victoria or London Bridge via Lewes in 1939 there were some 30 trains, 18 of which had Pullman cars. In 1984 there were 17 trains, of which 13 had a buffet. Journey times were rather slower than in 1939.

In the last few years there has been a progressive review of

Southern timetables that were originally based upon the Herbert Walker principle of strict adherence to regular interval working, with standardised departures easily memorised by regular passengers. Not all these reviews have had very happy results, despite the assistance of a computer. The Walker maxim 'To Brighton, every hour, on the hour, in the hour' – a marvellous selling point – has been abandoned. Today's London–Brighton timetable is, like Victoria Station concourse, something of a mess.

Elsewhere the time-honoured departure of the Portsmouth fast trains from Waterloo at 50 minutes past the hour has been changed to 48 minutes past for various off-peak services, thereby spoiling the pattern and ensuring that some passengers will miss their trains.

An example of the objective of achieving paper savings through reducing train mileage was the 1977 recasting of the Waterloo – Portsmouth timetable. That involved the withdrawal of all non-stop services between Guildford and London, and the cancellation of the fast trains to Portsmouth leaving Waterloo at 20 minutes past the hour. It led to objections from the principal towns along the line; Portsmouth City Council was particularly upset and protested, but without effect. However, the staff also threatened industrial action. The drivers were incensed because the reduced train mileage would affect their earnings. The Region thereupon conceded the extension of a Waterloo–Guildford stopping train as far as Portsmouth to boost the mileage and earnings for the sake of peace.

A side-effect of these timetable changes was that the stock working diagrams, which had provided main-line vehicles – Class 421 (4CIG and 4BIG) – on the regular-interval fast trains, with the much less suitable Class 423 (4VEP) stock with suburban pattern five-a-side seating and side doors confined to the stopping and extra peak hour semi-fast services, seemed to go by the board. An important evening Portsmouth train might include a 2HAP set, unsuitable for a 74-mile journey. Former 12-car formations were liable to be cut down to eight cars and occasionally even to four cars, with consequent overcrowding.

The shortening of trains on which Awayday tickets are available in many cases imported the crowding and discomfort

84

APT performed so well in experimental form . . . *(British Rail)*
. . . that the later snags were a great disappointment. Here, a test
formation of electric APT vehicles is propelled into sidings after 1984
trials on the East Coast Main Line between York and Northallerton.
(Ian S. Carr)

Southern priorities: superb modern technology in the new London Bridge signalbox . . . *(British Rail)*
. . . but no money to repair long-standing accident damage at Guildford station, Platform 1 *(Author)*

of peak hour travel into off-peak travel. As the latter is largely optional, and more susceptible to coach competition, the result was commercially unfortunate.

Above all, however, it was the sense of timing that was odd, because 1977 was around the time when the improved A3 (virtually a motorway) from Guildford to London was brought into use. National Express soon speeded up its competitive coach services; motorists from Petersfield, Haslemere, Godalming and Guildford suddenly found that the journey by car to London was far quicker and far less tiring than before.

What then are the reasons for this contrast between the Southern of pre-war days and the problem Region of BR today? Sir John Elliot has explained in his fascinating autobiography *On and Off the Rails* that the very effectiveness of Walker's modernisation of the Southern Railway penalised the Southern Region after nationalisation for a time, because the Railway Executive decided that the most urgent needs for post-war rehabilitation lay elsewhere, especially on the Eastern and London Midland Regions. The Board of the Southern Railway had approved in 1947, despite the prospect of nationalisation, a plan for electrification of all the main lines east of the Reading/Portsmouth axis, with diesel traction on subsidiary lines. This was laid aside by the Executive. Sir John has written: 'Missenden sent for me and said "The Southern have had all they're going to get for the time being. The emphasis must be given to the long-distance freight traffic" . . . It was a miserable existence'.

But even within these disheartening restrictions, the Walker legacy continued to impart some momentum, and, for a time, pride in a quality service. While Elliot was Chief Regional Officer at Waterloo (as the top post was then designated) Pullman services and named trains returned; something like the pre-war standard of cleanliness and punctuality was regained. Later on, much energy went into remodelling the electric power supply, and extending platforms to take 10-car trains to relieve overcrowding in the South Eastern suburbs. And then at last, under the 1955 Modernisation Plan, much of the pre-nationalisation plan for extension of electrification, now to Bournemouth, as well as to the Kent Coast by both the Chatham and South Eastern routes, was carried through, largely on 'Walker' principles.

Credit must also be given to the Southern for the rebuilding of the war-damaged Cannon Street and Holborn Viaduct stations, in association with privately financed office development, in a practical, no-nonsense standard of design. More recently, London Bridge, also largely a war casualty, has been rebuilt and much improved.

Criticism of the Southern however tends to be fixed mostly upon rolling stock – the thing the passenger most notices. The original electric stock provided before the second world war for Walker's suburban electrification schemes had been in line with contemporary standards; indeed much of it was converted steam stock. By the 1950s something more advanced was to be expected. After the delays referred to by Sir John Elliot, the Southern eventually received authorisation for quite a large renewal of pre-war vehicles but the first suburban stock replacements were the Class 405 (4SUB) units, an unhappy compromise between compartment and saloon design, rough riding and draughty; they were withdrawn, unlamented, in the early 1980s. The next series (from 1951) the Class 415 (4EPB), had similar characteristics and, despite a number having been face-lifted, remain in service as an old-fashioned design. The outer suburban Class 414 (2HAP) sets, including first class compartments and a lavatory, are a little better but still rough-riding at all speeds over 60mph.

The post-war main line stock built for the Southern's extensions of electrification to Bournemouth on the South Western Division and for the two Kent Coast electrifications, comprising the Class 410 (4BEP) sets, the Class 411 (4CEP) sets and the Class 491 (4TC) and Class 430 (4REP) were not examples of advanced design thinking – indeed the latter classes were adapted from locomotive hauled stock. The bogies of the former were always unsatisfactory, from the BR Mark I, largely based on the Southern's 'Eastleigh' bogie fitted to electric stock before nationalisation, to the modified Mark II, Mark III, and Mark IV designs. Complaints of bad riding after any substantial mileage had been run led to a decision to fit Commonwealth bogies for the stock designed for the second stage of the Kent Coast electrification; but this proved to be only a partial solution.

It was reasonable to hope that the new main line stock introduced from 1965 onward, Classes 420 and 421 (4BIG and 4CIG) would show more modern design ideas. To some extent this was certainly the case, and when new out of shops this stock with its later B4 type bogies rode much better than the pre-war 'Nelson' stock on the Waterloo–Portsmouth line or the elderly sets on the Brighton line which it replaced, and was welcomed by passengers on both these routes. But sadly, as service mileages increased, the riding deteriorated at speeds over about 60mph.

There is no doubt a good deal to be argued in favour of the refurbishing of the Kent Coast stock (Class 411, 4CEP), which costs less than replacement. The interiors are bright and attractive, but unfortunately the riding quality is still unsatisfactory at speed.

In 1967 came the introduction of Class 423 (4VEP) stock of which very large numbers were built for general use; no fewer than 193 units (772 vehicles) are on the stock list at the time of writing. The five-a-side second class seating is constricted for long journeys; the central passageway is barely wide enough to walk through; the first class compartments have slam doors that rattle and admit draughts; there is a curious mixture of internal and external door handles; and the riding is bad at speed. It will be sad if the commuters on the Charing Cross–Hastings route after electrification receive, in place of their superannuated diesel multiple-unit sets now stripped of their buffet service, nothing better than Class 423s.

The arrival of the Class 508 (later to depart for Merseyside) and Class 455 open saloon stock, light and modern in interior design, with power doors (60 years after the Underground introduced them) was very welcome, although it is a pity that some seats do not align with windows; riding was very greatly improved and the commuters of Chessington, Hampton Court and the Kingston roundabout much appreciated the new trains. But these routes are not heavily loaded in comparison with those of the South Eastern lines; one wonders why priority was given to them for new stock, rather than to the desperately overcrowded commuter routes of South East London and Kent?

The Southern, by far the largest element in the London &

South East Sector, is required to make economies to reach the financial target for the Sector, imposed by the Government. It has considerable scope for doing this. For a start its huge inner suburban traffic can be carried in trains with a single train operator. Guards are unnecessary, provided that power-door stock with a public address system replaces the slam-door stock still rattling around the system.

Hitherto the Southern has made no progress in this direction; the Class 455 sets on the Waterloo suburban lines still employ guards, although the London Midland Region's Moorgate–St Pancras–Bedford services operated by the 25kV ac version of the Class 455, Class 317, are one-man operated. Perhaps the most obvious case where guards are unnecessary is the Waterloo–Bank shuttle. If ever there is a case for driver only operation (DOO) that is it. And if DOO is achieved with no compulsory redundancy but reliance upon natural wastage, it would not be unreasonable to hope for staff and union acceptance.

On the Continental services, the Southern seems to have connived at Sealink's policy of down-grading the 'classic' passenger compared with the roll-on, roll-off motorist, by reducing the former boat trains to virtually commuter standard. This is a case where electrification has made life simpler for the operators but has not improved service to the passenger. Anyone who remembers the dedicated stock used for Continental services in steam days, kept in excellent shape at Grosvenor Road depot outside Victoria, will agree that the riding and amenities of the replacement stock are inferior. And as far as the withdrawal of all catering services is concerned, when one recalls the Pullmans with their elegant tables and pink-shaded lights, their excellent catering – not, incidentally, confined to first class passengers, as a corridor service was often also provided – the contrast is depressing, not merely in regard to the glamour trains, the Golden Arrow and the Night Ferry, but the regular run of Continental services upon which the Southern used to maintain an excellent standard of service.

It will no doubt be said that the traffic has moved down-market; that the students and schoolchildren who have so largely replaced the former business travellers do not demand such high standards. But there could be a vicious spiral, with lower standards reacting on patronage. Certainly one hears severe criticisms from passengers who have crossed Europe in, say, a smooth-riding modern DB carriage and are then jolted up to London in a Southern emu.

The Southern came rather late to accept that airline passengers could also be worthwhile train passengers. It was unfortunate that earlier on it had killed off a proposed Victoria-Heathrow direct rail link. BR headquarters and the Southern set up a Working Party in 1956 to study this project. The team identified an effective route from Victoria via Clapham Junction, Barnes, the Hounslow loop and a short spur from the Feltham area into the central terminal area, ending in a convenient sub-surface station. A warning was given by the airport authorities to reach a decision quickly as construction of the second runway would start before long and that would rule out cut-and-cover construction for the rail tunnel, which would be much cheaper than a deep-level bore. London might have gained something that Continental cities such as Frankfurt and Düsseldorf today enjoy, namely a rapid rail connection to and from its airport, instead of what eventually has been provided – a tube connection taking twice as long on the journey (18 stops from Piccadilly to Heathrow) with airline passengers sharing Spartan accommodation with straphanging commuters.

The scheme looked excellent. But the Southern operating department, oblivious to the decline in freight that was already setting in and unwilling to make adjustments to the timings of the sparse passenger service around the Hounslow loop, had insisted upon some quadrupling of that line, with a new Thames bridge. This damaged the scheme too much on cost grounds; a great opportunity was missed by the (then) British Transport Commission. In consequence, in 1983, BR only handled 3 per cent of Heathrow passengers against 36 per cent of Gatwick's.

In later years BR have accepted the need to cater for Heathrow by the institution of the Woking–Heathrow coach service, the Reading – Heathrow coach service and other experiments from Feltham and Iver. But these are poor substitutes for what might have been. The Southern has now seen the light so far as airline traffic is concerned and the zeal of the convert has almost, one suspects, led it to exaggerate the potentialities of the Gatwick traffic. Almost all through trains to and from the coast now stop at the excellently re-designed Gatwick Airport station. The new Gatwick Express service, from Victoria, four times an hour with Mark II air conditioned stock and a Class 73 electric locomotive, operating as push-pull sets, is in principle a good concept; but the average load factor so far is too low. And with the Southern so starved of modern, smooth-riding stock for its principal services, one wonders whether the Gatwick stock, representing an investment of £9 millions, might not have been better used elsewhere. The transfer of this service to the Inter-City Sector was announced as this book went to press. Significant?

When (Sir) John Elliot was Chairman of the Railway Executive, he made it clear that any proposal for new carriage stabling facilities was unlikely to get past the Chairman unless it incorporated a washing machine. J.E. had been brought up on the Southern Railway under Sir Herbert Walker and believed strongly that (train) cleanliness was next to godliness. The Southern had had a good record in this respect, and usually, pre-war, could put to shame the sprawling, too often grubby LMS. Sadly, that does not happen today.

The counterpart of external carriage washing is interior cleanliness, above all the thorough cleaning and restocking of lavatories with particular attention to refilling water tanks. One must accept that the quick modern turnrounds in terminal stations militate against proper cleaning. What is the remedy? More cleaners, perhaps even travelling cleaners may be the only answer.

What does this, on balance, rather depressing account add up to? It can be suggested that after the initial severe rationing of investment on the Southern under the Railway Executive, top management has felt it necessary loyally to support the views of the departments – especially operating and engineering – whose thinking may have been sound in purely departmental terms but did not collectively enable the Region to keep up with progress elsewhere in BR. Not that the individual chief executives at Waterloo since the 1950s can be criticised for this state of affairs; all have been under pressures unknown to their predecessors and have not been left long enough on the Southern to acquire the sort of detailed knowledge that Walker, Szlumper, Missenden or Elliot possessed. Strolling around Waterloo, Walker could walk into the 'A' signalbox, as his biographer C. F. Klapper relates, and astonish those on duty by correctly signalling a train's departure. Walker was 'down the line' for a full day at least once a week with a note-taking entourage, looking at everything and greeting everyone by name, noting shortcomings great and small which called for remedial action. On his return to the office he would dictate notes requiring action forthwith; major problems would be raised at the next Traffic Officers' Conference.

But then Walker had been General Manager of the Southern's largest constituent company for some 11 years and was in charge of the Southern for some 15 years thereafter. His experience thus was vast, and so was his consequential ability to dominate the departmental chiefs whenever necessary.

Under BR in recent years, the General Managership of the Southern has been recognised to be something of a crown of thorns, offering far more kicks than ha'pence. Partly therefore as an act of clemency and partly as a part of planned career development, it has represented only a passing phase in the progress upwards of the able and indeed distinguished people who have in quick succession occupied that difficult post at Waterloo.

What, if Sir Herbert Walker were in the saddle today, would he do? He might ask awkward questions about exactly what the passenger was going to gain from the huge resignalling of the Brighton main line and that technological marvel, the new Victoria signalbox. He might have spent that £120 millions upon better rolling stock, and upon cleaning and face-lifting a number of stations which are black spots.

He might also turn his attention to train catering and ask why the buffet cars seem to offer less choice and be often less inviting than those on other Regions. He might look at the total absence of catering on the South Eastern lines, including all Continental services. Cleanliness of rolling stock might go down in his notebook as a matter to be raised urgently at his Traffic Conference. He would certainly have wanted to keep the sensible and easily remembered regular departures and interval services as much for their publicity value as for passenger convenience. Lastly, at the same time he might review the direction which economies are being effected – cuts in train mileage and in station staffing to an extent that encourages too many passengers to use their cars. He was always concerned about economy but he might look for this in ways that do not reduce the quality of passenger service – for instance in introducing one-man operation on the Southern's huge inner-suburban train services. Alternatively, he might of course decide to resign in despair!

6

The Shrunken System, and BR's Urban Fringes

From Beeching (1963) to Serpell (1983), report after report upon BR's economics has fallen into the error of imagining that, within a large, financially-supported rail network there must be a small, self-supporting or profitable system, struggling to get out. The Beeching exercise was, by implication, based upon this theory. Now BR certainly has shrunk dramatically, from 19,600 route-miles AN (ante-nationalisation) to 10,500 route-miles PP (post-Parker). Yet the ultimate goal remains elusive. Was lopping the branches no more than cutting out dead wood, to the presumed benefit of the tree, or did the loss of the branches' foliage weaken the main trunk?

While many of the long-vanished lines had really no reason for survival, the pressure to show quick results – politically inspired – led to inadequate time being allowed for sufficient examination of the implications of closing other lines or cutting back services. Consequently, decisions were taken which could have been different if all the options – simplified operating methods, possible support from local authorities and organisations, additional and more attractive services, had all been explored.

During the Beeching era, case after case had to be worked up rapidly to meet the demands from headquarters. This also applied to cost-cutting exercises; the singling of the Salisbury–Exeter line was carried out too drastically and some double track has since had to be restored, together with the re-opening of Templecombe, Feniton (Sidmouth Junction), and Pinhoe Stations.

The railway survives largely because it offers a comprehensive transport service. Cutting it down until it serves only specific pairs of points, or a limited range of freight terminals, is bound to drive away a lot of traffic that over the greater part of its journey uses existing facilities at purely marginal cost. Take the case of passengers from Gloucester and Cheltenham respectively 113 and 120 miles from London, formerly enjoying a through train service (remember the Cheltenham Flyer?). Many residents now ignore the offered alternative of taking a diesel multiple-unit calling at all stations to Swindon and changing there into an IC125 for Paddington. They prefer to drive their cars to the nearby motorway.

It was therefore good news in 1984 when a Conservative Secretary of State for Transport stated that the Government had no wish to see BR's network drastically reduced. If one can rely on this as reflecting long-term policy, consideration might well be given to ways of making the 'fringes' – the lines maintained only through the Public Service Obligation, or cut down by BR in service quality through the pursuit of economies in the Inter-City business – more attractive and thus better utilised. A good start was made when BR reviewed the 'Cardiff Valleys' local rail network and issued a discussion document outlining the possibilities of building two more stations for newly-developed residential areas improved services and the replacement of existing dmu sets by new ones with, probably, pay-train operation and automatic ticket vending machines at stations.

Now this excellent example of enterprise, like other Western Region developments in the shape of the 'Cornwall Railway' and the 'Cotswold Railway', can surely be followed in other areas. But the key factor may well be the extent to which elected local authorities can be persuaded to interest themselves – both organisationally and financially – in such a positive approach, rather than merely passing over some of their TSGs (Transport Supplementary Grants) to BR just to maintain the existing level of service.

This question of co-operation on the fringes reaches its climax in the Passenger Transport Executives, whose future apart from that of the Metropolitan Counties which have funded them must be uncertain for some time in view of yet another reorganisation of local government. BR's relationships with the 'magnificent seven' (Sir Peter Parker's phrase) have not always been magnificent, but now have settled down, within a wide range of variations. At one extreme comes the Tyne & Wear PTE whose Metro system incorporates 27 miles of ex-BR route and eight miles of new construction, about half of which is in tunnel. The trains are purpose-built single-manned lightweight electric units with rapid acceleration and braking, not just dedicated BR stock, and the PTE employs the railway staff just as it does the busmen. Early controversies over the creation of this major urban transport system have died away, and BR has faded out of the area's local services. At the other extreme come the West and South Yorkshire PTEs which are primarily bus undertakings and where BR operates much as it did before the PTE was created. It was significant that it was for use in these two PTE areas that BR put in hand the construction of the first 20 Class 141 railbuses, the four-wheeled and (by intention) relatively inexpensive, lightweight replacements for the conventional BR dmu used in South and West Yorkshire. History however has repeated itself, in that the production models involve much 'railway' heavy construction principles – largely upon safety grounds, partly perhaps through conservativism among BR engineers – and this does not appeal to bus-minded PTEs.

In the middle come examples of close co-operation between BR and the PTEs, notably on Merseyside and in Glasgow (Strathclyde). The 'Merseyrail' network embodies a new City loop linking the former BR routes east of the river with the former Wirral and Mersey Railway routes on the Cheshire side. New tunnel construction has not been on the same scale as at Tyne & Wear, but the system has been united and well defined; trains operate under the joint PTE and BR logos.

In Glasgow the former Subway and the BR electrified suburban network are quite happily married within the PTE organisation. The PTE was fortunate in that BR had electrified almost all the suburban lines very effectively in the 1960s and this gave a flying start to the new organisation.

The West Midlands and Greater Manchester on the other hand, although exercising great interest in the rail network, have not been able to invest substantially in extending it.

WMPTE has opened new stations at University, Five Ways and Longbridge, and has plans for other new stations and station improvements, a 'softly, softly' policy on the whole. Greater Manchester PTE toyed with the idea of a major North–South rail link between the two principal stations (the 'Pic-Vic' project) but has been unable to get it off the ground, finance being the chief obstacle. A cheaper solution, the 'Windsor Link' enabling Piccadilly Station to serve North West areas was approved by the DoT early in 1985.

What then is the real role of BR in the conurbations; is BR deeply involved, on its own account, only with the London commuter region? Of course, BR can export technical expertise to a PTE and BREL can tender to build its rolling stock if it wishes to own its own trains and not merely support BR's operations. But the question seems part of a larger issue: is there ever to be a true national urban transport policy, within which the role of the railways is to be clearly defined? If so, then the contribution of rail technology to solving or easing the problems outside London surely needs to be looked at, and special assistance given to those local authorities which are anxious to take advantage of rail's potential for reducing street congestion, noise and air pollution, but which lack the resources to bring forward major schemes. Abolition of the Metropolitan Counties will pose acute problems for regional transport but if it removes some political influence from the PTEs, that may be no bad thing. The gap might then have to be filled by more impetus and encouragement from the centre, as part of that long overdue and long awaited national transport policy.

7

Travellers–Fare:
BR Asset or Albatross?

Except for very short journeys, eating and drinking are an important accompaniment to travel. The advantages of not having to carry one's own victùals on a journey have been recognised from the days of the coaching inns to the age of the airlines. Today we have to ask ourselves whether Travellers–Fare is a real asset to BR's passenger business, or an albatross hung around its neck. Two recent developments are important. First, even before the 'privatisation' of the railway hotels, T–F had become a free-standing organisation, no longer two junior divisions of British Transport Hotels. Secondly, the competition is hotting up: the London–Glasgow airline shuttle, for instance, now serves food and drink to passengers even on such a short internal flight, while the long-distance coaches on motorways are embarking upon meal service.

By any standards, Travellers-Fare is a large business. Station catering, with a staff of 2,700, earned a profit of over £1½ millions in 1983. There are refreshment rooms at 223 stations, of which 60 are operated by contractors and the remainder by Travellers-Fare direct; to the latter must be added several 'bistros', some off-licence shops and a small number of 'Casey Jones' Burger bars and 'Croissant Bars'. The refreshment room standards vary widely, from the excellent Trips at Waterloo to the pretty depressing establishment at Kew Gardens. Overall this side of the business is consistently profitable, though its integration with the rail passenger business is clearly less than in the case of the captive customers who require food and drink while in motion. The problems therefore centre more around the latter.

Curiously enough, the station refreshment rooms, despite being more profitable, used to be the down-market end of the business, with their marble-top counters and sandwiches under glass bell covers, compared with the more glamorous dining cars of the principal expresses, or the Pullmans with their traditional lamps on the tables and the spotless uniforms of the attendants. The best aspects of the refreshment rooms were the station dining rooms, some going back to the days before restaurant cars, when trains stopped for a luncheon interval at places such as York. They were almost all good. One remembers with affection the Surrey Room at Waterloo, and the Marylebone dining room, where one could lunch well and reasonably, served by attentive waitresses.

In fact, Travellers-Fare has shown far more enterprise in improving station catering than in train catering. The excellent 'Europa Bistro' at Liverpool Street has received well-deserved Press commendation. The large number of Real Ales served at many station bars is another good feature. Coffee made there in percolators is of an acceptable standard as a rule – cream too usually being available, not just the thin cold milk in cartons that normally is alone available on the buffet cars. An excellent feature common to the rooms and the cars is a drinkable house wine in quarter-litres at a reasonable price.

The chief problem is the variation in standards. If all cafeterias were as good as, say, the Europa Bistro, there would be little to criticise. But some cafeterias and rooms still fall short of the acceptable, and a few have actually declined; at Cambridge (Eastern Region) years ago the cafeteria served excellent hot food from a small kitchen but today the new and rather garish place offers only a pathetically small choice from a microwave oven.

A uniform, reliable, consistent standard of food, service and prices was the hallmark of the famous Lyons tea-shops before the last war; it was also an outstanding virtue of the Pullman organisation, and the secret of Fred Harvey's nationwide reputation as the caterer who attracted countless passengers to use the Santa Fé railroad. It is still practiced today by all the really successful catering chains; it depends upon clear and well-understood management objectives, pursued through strict control of staff and monitoring of performance.

Travellers-Fare is by no means short of ideas, many of them good. It is chiefly the lack of consistency and the frequency of policy changes that detracts from its performance. At Waterloo Station, for instance, a bewildering series of changes in recent years led one to wonder just what T-F was up to. The capital costs of tearing down and rebuilding bars and cafeterias more than once must have been huge. Certainly, one end-product, today's Trips cafeteria, is a marked improvement on all its predecessors, but one wonders whether closer management supervision earlier on would not have made such radical changes and outlays unnecessary.

There have always been arguments in the railway world about the use of catering contractors. The great Sir Herbert Walker believed strongly that railwaymen should run trains, and leave catering to experts in that field. So the Southern Railway leased its hotels to catering firms and had agreements for train and station catering with the Pullman Car Company, with Bertrams, Spiers & Pond, and later with Frederick Hotels. These seemed in general to be excellent arrangements; the travelling public was well served and the railway obtained rents or a percentage of the profits.

The opposite policy was followed by the London Midland & Scottish Railway, which operated its own hotels, cars and refreshment rooms. So did the Great Western Railway, which had never forgotten the unwise contract it entered into at a very early stage in its history with the infamous Rigby over the Swindon refreshment rooms. The London & North Eastern Railway followed a middle course, providing most services itself but admitting a few Pullman services as well.

After nationalisation, the tendency was to make all catering an 'in-house' activity, originally through the Hotels Executive of the British Transport Commission, then through the Hotels Division of the BTC, then through British Transport Hotels Ltd, a subsidiary of the British Railways Board. This policy appealed to the Labour politicians who passed the Transport Act 1947, and to the trade unions who support large monolithic public enterprises on principle and object to any form of contracting-out. It was also a form of empire-building that led the Hotels Executive, very soon after nationalisation, to take over the catering on the Southern Region (Western Section) from Frederick Hotels.

A sad combination of management errors and union intransigence produced, between 1963 and 1972, the disintegration of the Pullman service, officially described as 'integration' within BT Hotels. The immediate cause was the refusal of the unions to co-operate in staffing the 'Blue Pullmans' on Regions that previously had had no agreements with the Pullman Company, the London Midland and the Western. They argued that this affected the jobs of restaurant car staff of the Region concerned, even though a promise of employment with Pullman for BR staff was given. But the real reason was the less favourable (from the union angle) Pullman agreement, and the ideological dislike of contractors. BR, which should have reached agreement with the unions *before* ordering the Blue Pullmans, gave way; BR standard conditions were conceded and the 'integration' of Pullman into BTH sealed its demise in the long term.

Train catering is today accepted as a net marketing cost by BR passenger management. A formal financial contract with BR requires the passenger business annually to specify the extent and level of catering required, at a cost then quoted by T-F to BR. Receipts are then split between BR and Travellers-Fare, with the gap between the predicted cost and BR's major share of receipts forming the net catering cost, and Travellers-Fare's minor share funding HQ management and central services cost. The net cost to BR has been held to £7 million annually and is being reduced.*

Now on the face of it this seems an eminently reasonable arrangement, recognising the inter-dependent nature of the tasks of transporting passengers and comforting them with food and drink, something always understood by the shipping and air lines, and beginning (to BR's detriment) to be appreciated by the long-distance coach companies.

But three questions stand out. First, are losses inevitable? Second, is the standard adequate? Third, need train catering be an in-house operation?

On the point of losses, a hard-hitting and interesting article

---

* Quoted from B.R. 'Railtalk'

Contrast the spacious Waterloo Station concourse, with its new terrazzo flooring . . . *(Author)*
. . . with the congestion at Victoria (it is hard to believe that from this platform the prestigious all-Pullman Golden Arrow formerly departed) *(Author)*

Marylebone station's train-shed in mid-afternoon: its emptiness explains
the closure proposal . . . *(Author)*
. . . but probably the listed façade will survive commercial redevelop-
ment *(Author)*

by a part-time Member of the British Railways Board in the *Guardian* on 9 June 1981 argued that virtually no country makes money on train catering, because 'travelling restaurants are cripplingly expensive to run. You may need three stewards and two cooks to cope with the breakfast demand on a train getting into London at 9 am. But what do you do with them after that?

'There is little demand for lunch, and none for tea or morning coffee. You cannot have staff who have clocked on at 5 am kicking their heels all day until dinner time, without running into rest period, work hours, and overtime problems. You could send them home, but home is now a hundred miles away, and you cannot expect them to travel that far in unpaid time'.

This may be true. But how does it square with the fact that, in the past, private caterers – the Pullman Car Company, Spiers & Pond, Frederick Hotels – were able to operate under these handicaps and make a profit shared with the railway? Does one merely blame the Catering Wages Act? If so, how do other caterers, who have to cope with the Act, survive? Is there an answer in the management structure of T-F?

It must be remembered that great entrepreneurs have devoted their lives' work to promoting rail travel through high standards of catering – Georges Nagelmackers who created Wagons-Lits; G. M. Pullman whose name is synonymous with luxury travel; Fred Harvey, who brought a lot of business to the Santa Fé railroad through the slogan 'Meals by Fred Harvey'. What, one wonders, would these tycoons have said to plastic cups, Maxpax coffee, and long queues at the buffet counter waiting to obtain a sandwich wrapped in polythene or a single grilled sausage on a cardboard plate?

There is of course much to be said on each side. Travellers-Fare has claimed that it provides catering on 840 trains each weekday, with 270 offering full meals, more than is done on all the railways of Western Europe put together. This is perhaps not comforting to those many Southern Region passengers who lack such facilities. It is curious that the Southern provides trains with catering facilities to Guildford (30 miles from London, 58,000 inhabitants) but not to the Medway towns (32/36 miles and 210,000); to Winchester (66 miles and 32,000) but not to Canterbury (61 miles and 36,000); to Bognor (68 miles and 35,000) but not to Folkestone/Dover (70–77 miles and 80,000); to Eastbourne (61 miles and 78,000) but not to Margate/Ramsgate (73/79 miles and 90,000). Do the residents of Kent have smaller appetites or less to spend than those of Surrey, Sussex and Hampshire? One would like to know the effect of such deprival in stimulating the coach competition to these important traffic centres.

Looking at rail travel in the general social context, the habit of taking holidays abroad and improved living standards have combined to produce a greater interest in, and appreciation of, food and drink. Ethnic restaurants and the habit of wine-drinking have become much more popular. Certainly the fast-escalating cost of restaurant meals has prevented a growth in restaurant eating on the scale common in most European countries but, to counter this, thousands of public houses today offer bar food that is well cooked and surprisingly varied, at very reasonable prices. Now a buffet car is simply a pub-cum-café on wheels; and its aim should be to offer a choice of eatables comparable with that of the pubs. But in fact the range is usually restricted to 'convenience foods' of limited interest.

The argument usually employed to justify the existing standards is that the public's taste has changed, the substantial dining car meals of former years being little in demand by comparison with light meals or snacks, and that rail travel has moved down-market, with most well-heeled business travellers using planes or cars in preference to trains. Lastly, there has been a great growth in purchasing power of the young, who tend to spend their money on snacks and sweets rather than main meals. All this is valid; but there is an interaction of supply and demand. One can easily under-rate the sophistication of the customer, witness the campaign for Real Ale which the brewers originally dismissed as a cranks' fad.

Every experienced traveller has observed the variation in standards of service, which seems largely to depend upon the chief steward's personality and his relationship with his crew. In one car, a long queue may be impatiently waiting at the buffet counter for service from a single harassed steward while his three colleagues are engaged in unhurriedly preparing and serving meals to a small handful of customers in the restaurant end of the car. In another, a praiseworthy effort may be made to carry coffee and sandwiches for sale the length of the train. A few (very few) cars now offer excellent filter coffee with cream in cartons; most adhere to Maxpax with merely cold milk. Some cars are working throughout the journey; some remain closed long after departure (very annoying for hungry customers) or may close long before arrival. (One recalls travelling from Bristol to Paddington on a train in which the buffet car was announced to be closing before reaching Swindon, with only one-third of the journey completed; on a journey from the West of England, the 'last call' came just after Westbury, 1 hour and 40 minutes before arrival time, though the timetable shows buffet services as open to Reading, giving the crew about 25 minutes to clear up and get ready for any subsequent trip.

Everyone can call to mind odd examples of staff surliness, offset by pleasant experiences of fatherly chief stewards or cheerful stewardesses. The emergence of the latter is particularly welcome; catering, as a personal service, suits the feminine temperament in many ways, including pride in a clean uniform and helpfulness towards passengers with young children. The unions are not delighted by women taking what have traditionally been male jobs, but modern anti-discrimination laws have had their effect at last.

At the shrunken up-market end of the business, efforts are still made to cater for those businessmen and others who take a main meal on a train. Good food and drink, consumed with the scenery passing rapidly outside the window, is one of life's more enjoyable experiences; it is a pity that it has become rarer. The main reason may lie in the popular belief that restaurant car food is too expensive and not interesting. Whereas before the war, whole families would take lunch in the dining car as a matter of course, the bill now frightens Father. One sees a majority of even first class passengers in many IC125s patronising the buffet counter.

In detail after detail, one cannot help feeling that a new look would help. The microwave ovens already in use enable quite a wide range of dishes to be stored in the freezer and served in a matter of minutes. So à la carte menus, to suit varied tastes and varied pockets, are now practicable. They are a commonplace on DSG's excellent catering cars in Germany; even the metre gauge dining cars on the Rhaetian Railway in Switzerland and those on the main lines run by SSG, the Swiss Dining Car

Company, have much the same sort of approach. Why therefore cannot we get away from the tradition of table d'hôte meals, too often confined to a limited range of main dish or cold meat and salad, to which passengers are still summoned by the ominous 'Last call for lunch'? Why should not passengers be invited to visit the restaurant car at any time during the journey, and order any dish on the menu that they desire? The answer is probably the attitude of the staff, too set in their ways. But re-training is a possibility.

T-F announced in 1983 that it proposed to move into 'modular catering' – 'a system of demountable interchangeable units, that can be pre-loaded with pre-prepared victuals ready for on-board service, and heated (where necessary) on relatively simple fixed equipment such as microwave ovens.'

The concept involved a complete separation of the types of service offered to first and second class passengers. The former would be based on perambulating trolleys, serving passengers at their seats, hot food having been cooked in T-F depots and reheated in microwave ovens in the kitchen areas of the new catering cars. Second class passengers would be served at the buffet counter.

This of course departed from the traditional practice of the unclassed restaurant car which allows those who have only second class tickets to enjoy the same meal facilities as those with first class seats. It seems now to be agreed that linking travel class with eating opportunities will lead to loss of potential revenue – it is something of a reversion to the old First and Third Class Refreshment Rooms that used to be seen at major stations.

Two other points arise. One remembers the abortive experiment in the 1950s with 'Frood' – frozen pre-packed meals, pioneered briefly by J. Lyons and Co, an experiment abandoned after trial by T-F's predecessor, the Hotels Executive. The second point is that in the past, both substantial meals and a choice of à la carte dishes used to be prepared in kitchens no larger than those in a modern TRUB vehicle. Why is this then impossible today? Can the railway not recruit or train chefs with the same abilities as those of 50 years ago? One would have thought that the catering industry had today *more* training establishments, and *more* attraction for young recruits, than 50 years ago, witness the splendid Westminster Catering School in London and the enthusiastic students that it houses, or the South Devon Technical College in Torquay, right among the catering establishments of the English Riviera, to name but two.

At the buffet car counter, the standard should be that of good public-house bar food, rather than the present tiny repertory. The microwave makes it possible to serve at least basket meals – scampi and chips, chicken and chips, baked potatoes, and so on – with minimal preparation.

Lastly, tea and coffee! Why, when the station cafeterias can serve quite acceptable coffee with cartons of cream, cannot all buffet cars do the same? And why is the customer inflicted with those wretched little plastic 'stirrers' instead of spoons? The difference in cost must be insignificant; both are disposable, not re-used.

Tea too, the great standby of the British nation. Some T-F cafeterias now serve pots of tea with milk and sugar on a small compact tray, easily carried. Tea is such form tastes quite different from powder tea in plastic cups. The standard objections to this on trains are the loss of crockery and the stricter portion control and accounting given by the pre-packed and portioned cups; but in a captive environment such as a train surely this can be countered if the staff are willing to walk through the train before arrival at destination and collect the crockery. (At present certain crews are diligent in collecting used utensils and litter in their cars before the end of the journey: others are not).

In an organisation as far-flung as T-F, supervision on the ground is the key factor. So should not more inspectors be constantly travelling (not confining themselves to any one Region, where they would be quickly spotted) to see for themselves exactly what sort of service the ordinary member of the public is receiving. Undoubtedly quite a number of commendations, and not just criticisms, would flow from their reports, because there are excellent chief stewards and excellent crews, whose performance is limited only by management policy on supplies. There are also a few who are not really suited to this class of work, their attitude to the job being unfortunate, and who could perhaps be transferred to work not involving contact with the public.

At this point reference must reluctantly be made to 'fiddling' by staff. The first point is that the great majority are honest, hard-working people, though in any large flock there are bound to be a few black sheep. This is not the sole affliction of the railways or T-F, for they are found in all walks of life. It is alas a fact that cases of fiddling in T-F brought to court seem to receive a disproportionate amount of publicity compared with what would be given to similar cases of small dishonesty uncovered in a private firm. That is part of the general media delight in 'knocking' any nationalised industry. It is well known that in catering there are widespread 'customary practices', often silently tolerated by managements so long as they are kept within limits, that come close to 'fiddling' as understood elsewhere. Hotel chefs may receive secret commissions from suppliers. Some items of food are taken away as perquisites by staff; and bills to customers can be 'adjusted'.

Restaurant car meals, even though a bill is issued, can be a source of loss to the management if, for instance, the carbon copy of the bill used for control purposes is surreptitiously blanked off when the bill is written, so that later on a lower figure can be entered on the carbon and the staff can retain the difference between this and the amount paid by the customer. If bills are not torn across in the presence of the customer but merely crumpled up after payment, they can be retrieved, ironed out at home and later on placed in the pad and re-used.

Travellers-Fare has made strong efforts to check a practice that was formerly too prevalent – namely sales by staff of supplies brought in by themselves. Spirits and other beverages were the most common field for such fidding. Unfortunately the preventive measures have not always yielded a benefit to the passenger, witness the introduction of plastic disposable cups with pre-packed instant tea or coffee. This certainly made it more difficult for staff to sell their own coffee powder or teabags, but not impossible; used cups can be collected, washed in the kitchen and filled with powder for re-use. And the displacement of bottles of spirits dispensed through optics by miniatures of gin, whisky and brandy, with the object of stopping fiddling, may be effective but it means that one cannot buy a 'single' such as every pub supplies; sales to people unwilling to buy expensive doubles must be lost.

A slightly humorous footnote to the depressing subject of fiddling once came from a restaurant car superintendent. He complained that the British Transport Police when on the track of a particular crew all too frequently pounced on the offenders and laid charges (with the result that the crew were suspended from duty) immediately before a bank holiday, so that heavily loaded trains had to run without their advertised catering facilities. He asked why the arrests could not have been made on the Tuesday after the holiday, instead of the Friday before it!

What of the future? Travellers-Fare as a whole has been on the market under the privatisation policy, but the major catering chains decided in 1984 against any takeover. It may be that different treatment would be appropriate as between the station catering and train catering services. The former could be split into groups corresponding to the Regions and formed into companies, with a responsibility to the Regional General Manager for maintenance of standards to the public. Travellers-Fare announced in 1983 that a re-grouping had taken place, but that it had broken away from BR regional boundaries. (That may have spelt another instalment of UDI by the catering business which is not in the long-term interest of BR's passenger business.) Regional rather than Sector responsibility would seem to be more appropriate, because at so many stations the customers are not necessarily identified with any Sector; Inter-City, commuters, PTE, and Provincial service passengers may all mingle in the bars and cafeterias. Such groups, with an arithmetical average of under 50 station rooms each, would be reasonably 'manageable' so far as personal supervision and frequent inspection were concerned.

But train catering is a different matter. It is identified with the Inter-City Sector and should be made more responsible to it. Again, group management should be strengthened and the responsibility to provide services acceptable to the Sector Director made absolutely clear. Essentially, the groups should be small enough for really close contact between management and staff, each chief steward being personally known to management as were the former Pullman Conductors. That means service grouping as, for example, London–Manchester–

111

Liverpool; London–Birmingham–Wolverhampton; London–South Wales; London–Norwich. The name of the catering manager for each group (with his address and telephone number) should be prominently printed on every tariff card and menu and displayed at the buffet counter.

Despite the fact that the largest catering chains were not interested in making takeover bids, there could be enterprising catering managements of middling size that would be prepared to take up a contract and inject new ideas – above all in staff training and control – in ways that would be an asset to the passenger business. Ever since nationalisation, the railways have been stuck with a somewhat top-heavy, in-house organisation; thus they have been unable to compare performance with what an outside caterer might achieve, and equally unable to impose any sanctions if they fail to obtain the quality of service that promotes the passenger business. The result has been something of an albatross hung around BR's neck.

Summing up, while much that is praiseworthy in the Travellers-Fare approach to station catering should be acknowledged (the main problem being the need to bring the less satisfactory establishments in line with the best ones), there is scope and indeed a need for new thought and possibly new management techniques in train catering.

8

What Sort of a Ministry?

British Rail's sponsoring Ministry, the Department of Transport, has had a curious history, marked by many vicissitudes. Between May 1919 and the end of 1983 there were no fewer than 34 Ministers concerned with transport, an average tenure of about 1 year 11 months. Nor have the titles even been consistent: they have fluctuated between Minister of Transport, Minister of War Transport, Minister of Transport & Civil Aviation, Minister for Transport Industries, Minister for Transport, Secretary of State for Transport. Comparing this changing situation with that of the more senior Government posts such as Chancellor of the Exchequer or Home Secretary suggests that the role of the Department has never been fully clarified and that its headship has been regarded as either a stepping-stone to higher office or a backwater into which a politician can be safety shunted.

Many have complained that Britain has never, except briefly during the two world wars, enjoyed a national transport policy. Our rulers have seldom been able to make up their minds about the right quantity, quality and type of transport that the nation requires and can afford. Political dogma also has too often invaded the subject and legislation has seldom been based upon sufficiently objective studies of needs and resources. At the end of World War I there was a fleeting prospect that the Government would create a Department able to plan and execute a national transport policy. The dynamic Sir Eric Geddes, who had been Deputy General Manager of the North Eastern Railway up to the outbreak of hostilities in 1914, had entered the wartime service of the Government, originally as Deputy Director General of Munitions Supply, in which capacity he had greatly impressed Lloyd George. His rise thereafter had been meteoric: to Director-General of Transportation in 1916, First Lord of the Admiralty in 1917, and Minister without Portfolio in charge of post-war demobilisation in 1918. In the brief euphoria of post-war planning, Geddes was asked to organise transport, and in February 1919 he put forward to the Cabinet a Bill for a Ministry of Ways and Communications that would own or control railways, roads, ports, canals, shipping, air transport and electricity generation. Air transport was immediately deleted by the Cabinet (there was not to be a combined Ministry of Transport & Civil Aviation until after 1953). Shipping was left with the Board of Trade after a tussle with the President of the Board, Sir Albert Stanley, the future Lord Ashfield. The electricity powers (which Geddes wanted largely because of his far-reaching ideas about main line railway electrification) were also drastically cut down.

Even so, there was a possibility that the new Ministry (renamed by the House of Lords the Ministry of Transport) might nationalise the railways, with Geddes as the railway 'supremo' being also in charge of the national road building programme. In June 1920 this was finally decided against at a Cabinet meeting, though only after the new Ministry had been set up in August 1919. Geddes was thus left to develop proposals for grouping the railways under continued private ownership which he did in the much-criticised Railways Act of 1921.

Since that time the Ministry has seldom come close to evolving a national transport policy. For most of the period the Ministry has had a regulatory rather than an operational function, except in wartime. Ministers were, on the whole, birds of passage and, apart perhaps from Geddes, Herbert Morrison, and Barbara Castle, have not been imbued with strong personal convictions about transport.

For most of the inter-war years the Permanent Secretary since 1926, Sir Cyril Hurcomb, was a distinguished and capable civil servant but also one endowed with a very strong streak of caution. To be fair, however, between the wars the Ministry did produce two major Acts intended to rationalise in some measure the relations between road and rail transport – the Road Traffic Act of 1930 and the Road and Rail Traffic Act of 1933. The former introduced service licensing of bus and coach operations; the second, quantity licensing of commercial road haulage. Both measures have been criticised by economists as too restrictive, but they introduced some stability and some guarantee of consistent public service into industries that had grown rapidly but very unevenly. Lastly, the Ministry sponsored the Act that was Herbert Morrison's brainchild, the London Passenger Transport Act of 1933 which pioneered the idea of locally 'integrated' passenger transport embracing road and rail.

None of these measures however was based on comprehensive thinking about just how transport as a whole could best serve the needs of the nation. The chance that Geddes had missed seemed fleetingly to reappear in 1945 when a Labour Government came to power with even more radical ideas of changing the social and economic structure of the country than those that had briefly flourished in 1919. The Ministry of Transport was at last set to work, to nationalise and reorganise public transport from top to bottom. Alfred Barnes, the Minister of Transport under Attlee was, like many of his predecessors, without any background in transport; he came from the Co-operative Movement. He was on the whole a practical man rather than a Socialist with dogmatic convictions. But he was sandwiched between Herbert Morrison, who was in charge of the Attlee Government's socialisation of industries programme, and his very experienced Permanent Secretary, Hurcomb. Morrison was convinced that a system of public Boards, appointed by and generally accountable to Ministers, but free from detailed control in their business operations, was the only way to carry socialisation into effect. After all it had worked well, it seemed, in London Transport. Hence the creation under the 1947 Transport Act of the huge British Transport Commission intended to 'integrate' all public inland transport – just how, was never explained. Railways and canals were taken over at a stroke, together with London Transport and all the railways' subsidiary interests – shipping, hotels and investments in road transport. Road haulage was to follow.

A consequence not fully realised at the time was that the Ministry of Transport lost, instead of gaining close contact with the railways. Even under private ownership in wartime the

Ministry had exercised control through the Railway Executive Committee which continued to exist until the Transport Commission was set up. Before the war, too, the railways had had regular contacts with the Ministry about their problems and their relationship with road transport. They had been represented on the Minister's Transport Advisory Council and on special bodies such as the Salter Conference on Road and Rail Transport, not to mention having given evidence at great length to the Royal Commission on Transport, 1929–31.

Suddenly after nationalisation the relationships became more of an arm's length one. All railway contacts with the Ministry had to be channelled through the British Transport Commission, something that neither the Minister nor the railways relished, but which was insisted upon by Sir Cyril Hurcomb, who had now become the Comission's Chairman. And this distancing of the railways from the Government, this attitude that, although the railways belong to the State, the State has no direct responsibility for them (so that if they are in difficulties, it is probably their own fault!) has persisted to this day. It has survived the break-up of the Transport Commission and the transfer of the railways to the British Railways Board – which in theory, as the Board is appointed directly by the Minister and there is no intervening Commission, should have brought relationships closer.

But no; the Ministry stands back as an observer and critic of the performance of the railways which it owns. Paradoxically enough, this has occurred at a time when the Ministry (Department, since 1970) has at last acquired nearly all, instead of merely a selection, of the functions implied by its title. For many years it was anomalous that shipping rested with the (former) Board of Trade and civil air transport with the Air Ministry: Geddes's emasculated Ministry of 1919 seemed to have inherited little beyond the Railway Inspectorate of the Board of Trade and the former Roads Board. Gradually this has been largely rectified; today's Department of Transport covers land, sea and air transport. It is responsible for the nationalised railways, airlines and bus network. It covers shipping and ports, and in road transport it embraces the construction and maintenance of motorways and trunk roads, the licensing of motor vehicles and the oversight of the transport planning of local authorities including the payment of central Government grants to them.

This formerly rather junior Ministry now via four deputy secretaries exercises its great range of functions through some 16 under-secretaries who are directly concerned with transport (there are others in finance, liaison, etc.), and no fewer than 45 assistant secretaries and 14 senior specialists such as chief engineers. There is thus an impressive assembly of the higher talent of the civil service in No 2 Marsham Street, Westminster. But out of the 16 under-secretaries, only two concern themselves with railways; of the 45 assistant secretaries, only four are involved. In contrast, seven under-secretaries deal with roads and motor transport, supported by 13 assistant secretaries and eight chief experts.

Still, it is only in the realm of trunk roads that the Department exercises a truly creative role. In the case of motorways the policy, the planning, the design, the land acquisitions, the public consultation processes, and the letting of contracts for the physical construction are all in the hands of civil servants. Central policy for all trunk roads is laid down centrally; its execution is entrusted either to highway authorities or to the Department's own Road Construction Units (RCUs). The latter were originally set up by Mrs Barbara Castle when she was Minister to cope with the flood of new work created by the decision to construct 1,000 miles of motorway within a decade or so.

With this major exception, the Ministry is essentially a regulatory body, examining, criticising and legislating for the forms of inland transport by rail, road haulage, passenger service vehicles, private cars and motor cycles. It is only creative, only able to achieve direct physical results, in its road building programmes. Everything else is either in the private sector or in the hands of nationalised public Boards such as the BRB, with whom the relationship is an arm's-length one.

Here lies the crux of the matter. The Ministry is bound to be responsive to the inter-relationship between roads and road users. Building motorways stimulates road traffic. It suggests that heavier freight vehicles and faster-moving coaches can safely be authorised and Ministerial decisions giving effect to this follow on. On the other hand, the Ministry has never initiated proposals for railway development. Its civil servants merely monitor the performance of British Rail, comment upon it and make recommendations to their Minister upon it.

Civil servants are highly trained in the techniques of detecting weak points in any document submitted to them. Consequently, they are not fulfilling themselves if they tamely endorse proposals coming from BR. But where does the detection of major weaknesses or possible conflict with Government policy end and where does mere nit-picking begin? Many investment decisions involve considerations that cannot easily be quantified, and this is recognised in road construction.

Would it not have been better, assuming that the railways were to be nationalised, to involve the Ministry more directly in their problems and their performance? Should not the fact that the British taxpayer has purchased at considerable cost a major asset in the shape of British Rail induce the servants of the State to protect the State's investment as far as is reasonably possible? They should not of course seek restrictions that might be detrimental to the economy or the environment; a balance must be struck. But when one is reminded that tax-payers' money has gone into the railways, one recalls how much has also been laid out in building a toll-free motorway network which obviously erodes the traffic on the railways. In France and Italy the motorways have been self-financing, being subject to tolls which pay interest on the costs of construction and maintenance. Why not here?

Sometimes one arm of the British Government seems to act in ignorance or independence of what another arm is doing. For instance, around the time that the extension of the London Midland Region's electrification to Glasgow was approved by the Ministry of Transport, the Civil Aviation Authority approved the British Airways Heathrow–Glasgow shuttle service which badly damaged the financial justification for the rail electrification project without however eliminating the need for it.

Each form of transport of course lobbies and seeks to influence the Department. Curiously, however, it does appear from its actions that the Department (quite independently of the political allegiance of its Minister) is usually more receptive to the side that is predominantly private-sector than to the side that the Department has fathered and (on behalf of the nation) really owns. The decision to increase the permitted gross weight of articulated lorries from 32 tonnes to 38 tonnes is a good example. Another is the raising of speed limits for coaches, which obviously increases their potential for competing with British Rail. Were British Rail's objections to this heard at all? And what about the relationship between the damage caused to the roads, above all by heavy lorries, and the annual tax payable on such vehicles? Even in 1983, on the basis of figures prepared by the Department's own Transport and Road Research Laboratory, the tax shortfall was some £880 per vehicle per annum, and over the past 10 years the shortfall in respect of the fleet of such vehicles has totalled over £1,000 million at current prices – an enormous hidden subsidy from the taxpayer. An article in the *Times* by John Wardroper has commented: 'The damaging effect of big lorries in the real world of shaky bridges and lane closures is, indeed, not fully reckoned throughout the cost calculations. The Department bases its "damage factor" figures on what an annual sample of lorry operators *say* their lorries are carrying. Lorry men, filling in official questionnaires, do not confess to illegal overloads. The gap between fiction and reality can be large; if a lorry axle carries one ton over the legal limit it does nearly 50 per cent more damage.

'The Department has quantities of computerized figures on overloading. Analysis of data from sites on the M1 and A2 has shown that the damage being done by 32-ton lorries was 77 per cent greater than what the Department assumes for tax purposes. Yet the Department says it cannot see how to count any sum whatever for overloading.'

The total cost of road accidents in 1982 was reported by the Department to the House of Commons Transport Committee; it amounted to a staggering £2,370 millions. Of this, £900 millions was damage to vehicles and property; £720 millions the effect of death and injury on production; £560 millions was a notional figure for grief, pain and suffering; £120 millions for police and insurance; and £70 millions for ambulance and hospital costs. Road deaths were 6,000; serious injuries 80,000 and 249,000 slight injuries.

Compared with the impressive safety record of the railways (set out on page 7), these figures must surely establish a prima facie case for influencing the public to use rail transport as an alternative to the car, the coach or the lorry. But has there been any sign of a campaign by the Department?

Again, on the issue of costs; does the Department do anything to alert the motorist to the real cost of motoring? According to the motorists' own protection organisation, the Automobile Association, in April 1984 the true (as opposed to the motorist's perceived) costs of private car mileage varied as follows (based on petrol at the then £1.84 per gallon):–

Small car (engine capacity up to 1,000cc)
   Standing charges per mile in pence
      Based on 10,000 miles per annum   12.880p
   Running charges per mile,
      on 10,000 miles per annum   9.707p

                          Total cost per mile   22.587p

Ordinary family saloon (engine capacity 1001 to 1500cc)
   Standing charges per mile
      Based on 10,000 miles per annum   15.830p
   Running charges per mile
      on 10,000 miles per annum   10.538p

                          Total cost per mile   26.368p

Large company car (engine capacity 2001 to 3000cc)
   Standing charge per mile
      Based on 20,000 miles per annum   15.316p
   Running charges per mile
      on 20,000 miles per annum   17.875p

                          Total cost per mile   33.191p

The mileages shown for the small car and the family saloon are the normal averages of 10,000 per annum; the large company car can be expected to be used much more intensively and for longer journeys, so 20,000 miles has been assumed.

The total theoretical annual costs are thus far higher than the average motorist realises – £2,258 for the small runabout,

Two very different
personalities: *(left)* Sir
Herbert Walker who built up
the Southern . . . *(David
Lipson)*
. . . and *(below)* Dr Beeching
who cut down BR *(British
Rail)*

Tyne & Wear Metro train – a good case of BR/PTE collaboration in which the PTE took over some former BR routes and developed its own ideas *(Ian S. Carr)*

First attempt at a railbus for the PTEs, Class 141 *(British Rail)*

£2,637 for the average family saloon, and no less than £6,638 for the large company car!

Admittedly a reduction in the AA's figure of standing charges will be obtained by a high proportion of motorists. Maximum no-claim-bonuses could bring down the insurance costs; buying second-hand rather than new reduces depreciation and loss of interest; not all motorists pay the AA subscription of £35 pa, and the assumed costs of £156 for garage/parking fees can be reduced for many. But even so, the figures are sobering and may well lead to a fresh view of the comparative costs of private car and rail travel. If, for instance, an Awayday ticket is taken from Haslemere to Waterloo (43 miles) the 1984 fare was £4.90 for the 86-mile journey, out and home. The cost of petrol alone for a 1,500cc car was likely to be more than £5; to which parking fees in London must probably be added. The true running cost, excluding all standing charges, ie just petrol, oil, tyres, servicing and repairs, on the AA scale for the journey amounts to over £9, and the total theoretical mileage cost (which everyone of course disregards) would be £26.36 for a car averaging 10,000 miles a year. For the more heavily-used company car, the cost would be £28.59. But the motorist is about as far removed from 'economic man' as it is possible to be. His relationship with his car is an emotional one – an interesting psychological phenomena. (How many otherwise mild-mannered and inoffensive citizens, once behind the wheel, turn out to be aggressive drivers? Maybe psychiatrists should stop putting patients on a couch and instead put them in the driving seat and observe their behaviour towards other road users!).

A Department that was motivated to reducing the total social cost of providing the transport that the nation requires would surely attach weight to these considerations, especially since the problem of damage to highways and bridges caused by the uncontrolled growth of motor transport, above all by heavy goods vehicles, is now coming home to roost. It is clear that the motorway network inaugurated in the 1960s is requiring renewal far sooner than was anticipated at the time of construction, the most notorious example being of course the grossly overloaded M1. The drastic remedial measures needed on the Severn Bridge is another illustration – £33 millions just to avoid the risk of collapse, Even Hammersmith Bridge in London, on a relatively lightly-used route with about 37,000 vehicles a day, has had to be closed owing to serious damage largely caused by lorries which ignore the 12-tonne weight limit imposed over the bridge.

Under a Conservative administration, the Department appears to take the line that all use of the roads is entirely a matter of private judgment, an unalienable right with which it is not proper for Governments to interfere. Yet in other fields – such as the requirement for warnings about the danger to health from smoking to be included in cigarette advertising – the Government does accept that it has a responsibility to its citizens, to dissuade them from activities which are dangerous or involve excessive social costs. Why is this not done in transport? Road transport's responsibility for damage to the environment – buildings as well as human health – is vast. When smog afflicted the Ruhr in West Germany in January 1985 private motoring had to be temporarily forbidden.

An interesting note in *Country Life* (22 March 1984) recorded recently that 'The French Grégoire Commission have done research into how much the different modes of transport cost the taxpayer, Apparently, for each tonne-kilometre of freight moved, each French taxpayer contributes 18.7 centimes for carriage by water, 25.8 centimes for carriage by rail, and 61 centimes for carriage by road. For a comparison with Britain, take into account that the French railway deficit is between two and three times that of Britain, and also that a toll is payable for lorries to use the autoroutes.'

Moving towards a better balance between over-crowded roads and the often under-utilised railways *must* make good economic and social sense. It is not assisted by setting the railways financial targets difficult of attainment (except by reducing service quality and/or quantity) and by severely restricting investment. There are times when one feels that a better balance would have been achieved if the railways had not been put under a public board after nationalisation but directly under a Minister of Railways who – as in India – could have put their case and financial requirements directly to the Cabinet instead of through a Ministry whose main activities are concerned with other forms of transport.

9

The Limits of Privatisation

One of the characteristics of the civil service is the way in which it can devote itself to implementing diametrically opposed policies from time to time at the behest of the appropriate Minister. There is no consistent 'Department' policy for the ownership or organisation of transport; just as the industry was pretty comprehensively nationalised in 1948, in the 1980s much of it is being 'privatised'. Will the pendulum swing yet again? Steel has been nationalised, de-nationalised and re-nationalised. Transport has not yet become quite such a football, to be kicked backwards and forwards into first one goal and then the other; but reversing the actions of the Attlee Government of 1945–51 does seem to have been an objective of the Thatcher Government from 1979 onwards.

Privatisation has two faces, one quite a fair one and another a distinctly ugly one. The fair face derives from the argument that if private investors are willing to fund an enterprise, there is no reason why the State (ie the general body of taxpayers) should do so. The State should concern itself with questions of high policy at home and abroad; business is best left to businessmen. And business is most likely to be efficient when it is free from the dead hand of State bureaucracy, and is not confined to tasks and objectives laid down in Acts of Parliament. In fact, even a Socialist economist, an MP and former Labour Minister, has admitted that 'it is damaging to impose such inflexibility on public enterprise, because as soon as the economic wind changes, the private firm can branch out into new activities, but the public cannot'. (Douglas Jay, MP, *Socialism in the New Society*, 1962).

So the privatised business should be able to extract investment finance more easily from the stock market than the public corporation can from a suspicious and sceptical Treasury. It should be able to diversify, branching out into new and profitable activities wherever it sees a chance. And possibly (though this is debatable) it will attract more managerial talent than the public enterprise because of its greater flexibility in offering pay and fringe benefits comparable with those in competing industries.

The ugly face of privatisation is the Conservatives' doctrinaire objection to public ownership, as irrational in the setting of today's mixed economy as is Labour's doctrinaire demand for much more public ownership. This too often ignores the real problems of business, that have little to do with ownership, everything to do with markets, investment needs and industrial relations. The late Lord Crowther, equally distinguished as economist, journalist and business leader, once said: 'The issue of public or private enterprise is irrelevant. It is the quality and quantity of enterprise that is important.' Tit-for-tat legislation, the pendulum swing of changing ownership enforced by the two main political parties during the past four decades, has too often been an irrelevancy and sometimes a damaging one.

Another unpleasant feature of privatisation is discernible when the policy is applied to a conglomerate with some activities that are profitable and saleable and others that plainly are not. Enforced sales by BR of ancillary businesses can produce some useful cash in the short run but only at the expense of future income – and if the BRB External Financing Limit is reduced pro rata, there is no benefit to railway investment programmes as there should be.

There is admittedly no compelling reason why a railway should own hotels, do its own train and station catering, build its own rolling stock, or operate ships. Many railways, in many parts of the world, have left these functions to other concerns and have concentrated upon the business of running train services. Under nationalisation, there has been a process of hiving-off the so-called ancillary services from railway management under Governments of both the Left and the Right, though in the former case not to private enterprise but to 'splinter' public Boards.

The BRB has responded to political pressure in recent years

for disposals by setting up a wholly owned subsidiary company, British Rail Investments Ltd, to oversee the 'privatisation' process in a business-like way. The hotels and Sealink UK have been sold; the hotels were saleable largely upon site values and potential. Their disposal did not cause many tears to be shed, except perhaps among railway officers who had used them for many years and felt at home there, though ever since 1948, when the hotels were first taken away from direct railway management, the links with the railway had tended to weaken. Moreover, neither the Hotels Executive of the former British Transport Commission nor British Transport Hotels of the BRB had seemed to be entirely successful in coping with the legacy of Victorian buildings and heavy overhead costs bequeathed to them by the main line railway companies. Sir Herbert Walker of the Southern Railway always opposed any direct railway involvement; the opposite view was taken by the other three companies, partly because, quite apart from the original purpose of encouraging rail travel, it was convenient to have hotels always available for functions such as board dinners, entertainment of important traders by railway goods managers and messes for senior officers, and partly because the hotels provided a supply base for both refreshment rooms and restaurant cars, the administrations being neatly tied in. But severance of these links in recent years has been progressively completed.

The privatisation of station and train catering would be nothing new; there have always been divided opinions within the railways as to whether contractors, who could be replaced if unsatisfactory, might not be preferable to building up an in-house organisation which might become a strong vested interest within the management structure, hard to subordinate to the traffic needs of the railway.

The disposal of Sealink UK has been complicated by the fact that it is part of an international consortium, the other partners in which are predominantly State-owned. Equally, the implications of creating a monopoly on those routes (especially across the English Channel) which have become increasingly competitive in recent years, with benefit to users, was taken very seriously by any British Government; they led to the decision to exclude P&O and European Ferries from bidding for Sealink UK.

There was a general argument for Sealink's privatisation. Formerly the railway steamer services could be regarded as merely projections of train services; the packet ports were simply a form of railway station. But today the roll-on, roll-off business so dominates Sealink's finances that the rail passengers using the ships have become second-class citizens. They are, for instance, not allowed to disembark until the cars, lorries and coaches have driven off – and then they may have to board a bus to take them to the town's ordinary station and catch an ordinary train. It is a far cry from the pampered passengers on the Golden Arrow being whisked on to the *Canterbury* and whisked off on the other side of Channel into their waiting Pullmans. One may regret this, but it is a fact of life.

The railway workshops managed by British Rail Engineering Ltd are a difficult case. Their separation from the regional railway management has become progressively wider since 1963. The existence of BREL's joint marketing subsidiary with the sole remaining large manufacturer of railway rolling stock in this country, Metropolitan-Cammell, set up after 1968, might suggest that privatisation should be relatively easy. BR has in fact loosened the ties by inviting tenders from the private sector for some of its own new rolling stock. But there are two major problems. Despite BREL's ability to manufacture for export, BR remains, overwhelmingly, its most important customer, as well as its parent. And four-fifths of BREL's work is maintenance, with only one-fifth new construction. When the new arm's-length relationship was created, the arrangement was that work for BR would be charged on a 'full cost' basis, whereas work for outside customers was expected to yield a profit. A private owner of BREL, might, if pushing up prices to BR, face the loss of much business from his principal customer.

And, overall, a paradoxical situation has developed. It is unquestionably the case that BR is short of passenger stock in many areas. Apologies over the loud-speakers for Southern Region trains being cut from 12 to eight, or eight to four coaches 'owing to shortage of stock' are a commonplace occurrence for that Region's commuters. And the IC125 fleet is taxed to the limit to maintain its planned circuits, even though great ingenuity has been exercised in obtaining maximum utilisation. (Sometimes unrealistic targets have been set and have had to be reduced, as in the May 1984 timetable.)

The price that is being paid for intensive diagramming of this kind is increased annual mileages, in turn demanding a reduction in the time intervals between heavy repairs. It can also be argued that the too frequent experience of rough riding indicates that with today's intensive use of passenger stock the theoretical book lives need to be shortened. Overall, BR thus not merely needs additional vehicles, but the problems of excessive wear and tear, and also of obsolescence, loom large. The remaining Mark I locomotive-hauled vehicles are on their way out; before too long, locomotive-hauled stock for the East Coast electrification will be on the horizon. But even sooner, the huge dmu fleet built in the 1950s and 1960s and much Southern commuter stock will have to be replaced. There is a further demand for the rebuilding of stock in whose construction asbestos was used – dmu and emu alike, and it is quite formidable in total. Yet against this picture of immediate and future BR needs, BREL is short of orders so far as to involve staff redundancies and closures. If only the finance were available, surely much capacity claimed to be excessive could be taken up.

Were a private buyer to be found for BREL, with large financial resources, might it be possible to see a return to a practice of locomotive and rolling stock builders in the 19th century when orders were slack, building for BR on a basis of long credit or hire-purchase finance? (The provision on this basis of rolling stock for the Great Central Railway's London Extension comes to mind.) Overtaking arrears of replacement within BR and keeping BREL at full stretch might thereby be facilitated.

The British Rail Property Board can be considered as already effectively privatised, since its main activity is either selling off rail sites which have been identified as surplus to railway requirements, or developing them in partnership with a private developer. Many of the latter projects are planned to obtain much-needed railway station improvements without cost, or with greatly reduced cost to BR. Further privatisation might in fact increase BR's financing difficulties for station improvement in the long term.

Freightliners Ltd is a wholly-owned BRB subsidiary and as such could, in theory, be sold as a company. But it is not so long since it was recognised that the separation of Freightliners from the railway under the 1968 Transport Act had been a mistake; its return to railway control was welcomed in view of the close interworking with railway management that the Freightliner concept involves. Moreover, the company's financial performance has never reached the heights looked for in the 1960s.

Lastly comes the main question – what about the railway itself? After all, in 1983 the railway achieved a surplus of £64 millions before interest charges, etc, after grants totalling £934 millions from central Government and local authorities, and £24 millions grants for special purposes. If – and it is a very big 'if' – there was a guarantee that grants at this level would continue, might not a purchaser be interested in taking over the railway? One suspects that the whole complex of businesses – the five Sectors as identified in BR's management structure – would be impossible to market, but there are other possibilities that may be worth examining. One has already been mooted in the Press, the detaching of a section of railway that is relatively self-contained, ie the London, Tilbury & Southend section of the Eastern Region. Curiously enough, it was this former District which was identified by Sir Reginald Wilson when Chairman of the Eastern Area Board as the prototype for Line management below Regional level, a concept which he enthusiastically promoted and which worked well for a number of years. John Dedman as Line Manager, LT&S, Gerry Fiennes as Line Manager, Great Northern, and Willie Thorpe on the Great Eastern, all turned the concept of Line management into a success story.

The LT&S is still reasonably separable from the rest of BR. It was formerly a separate railway company until it was gobbled up by the Midland in 1912 under the nose of the Great Eastern. Its passenger service is almost entirely self-contained, apart from the odd special working. Its (still quite substantial) freight originating on Thames-side is largely transferred to other Regions at the Ripple Lane (Barking) Yard. Its costs are therefore fairly identifiable, as are its receipts. But it remains a doubtful proposition, since BR would almost certainly have to provide many services for a London, Tilbury & Southend Railway Company, perhaps on an agency basis; what, then, would be the point of privatisation?

Other possibilities exist, at any rate in theory. One is a form of partnership between the State and private enterprise, as was envisaged in the LNER 'landlord and tenant' scheme of 1947, put forward as an alternative to outright nationalisation. Under it the State would have acquired by purchase from the private railway companies the infrastructure – track, structures, signalling, etc – and would then have licensed the use of it in return for rental payments to the extent that these could be afforded by viable railway services. Today the State already owns the infrastructure, but the surplus on railway operating is insufficient to meet the costs of maintenance, let alone pay any 'rental'. But an ingenious alternative notion has been put forward in an article in *Transport*, the Journal of the Chartered Institute of Transport. The author suggests that the railway infrastructure should be maintained on exactly the same basis as the road system through financing by central and local Government. The central Government would maintain the major trunk routes (as it does motorways and trunk roads); secondary and minor lines would be maintained by local rates assisted by central Government grants-in-aid. Then, a tax would be levied, based upon gross weights on the same principles as apply to commercial road vehicles, on every rail locomotive, carriage and wagon. Subject to payment of the tax, these rail units would have unrestricted rights of user of the rail infrastructure.

Within this framework, private companies would be able to tender for franchises to operate particular groups of services; BR equally would be a possible operator for all or part of the network. The author wisely concludes his article with the caution that it 'makes no attempt to resolve the difficulties that would be created by its implementation'; these obviously would be formidable and perhaps insurmountable. The real value of the idea lies in the argument that the rail infrastructure is a national asset akin to the road infrastructure, and its upkeep could logically be treated in much the same way.

Perhaps the last aspect of privatisation that needs

consideration is the possibility of a take-over by managers and staff of BR on the lines of the successful takeover of the National Freight Consortium. The trades unions, who advised their members not to participate in the NFC scheme, are now sourly aware that their advice was bad; the minority who abstained are envious of the majority who took up shares which are now worth very much more than their purchase price. Sadly, however, one must doubt whether there is any scope on BR for such an operation. How could one value or fix a price for shares in a British Railways Company, since the prospect of any dividend must depend upon a guaranteed continuance of Public Service Obligation financial support – and no Government can tie down its successors? Ruling out BR as an entity, therefore, the prospects of a management/staff consortium would seem to be confined to individual sections that are viable; here the London, Tilbury & Southend line might just be a possibility. It would be an interesting experiment in introducing co-partnership into the railway world.

The other possibility, although it would not be privatisation, would be the much closer involvement of all local authorities in the financing and running of sectors of the railway within their areas – not just in the areas of the Passenger Transport Executives created by the 1968 Act, or the TSG payments of Shire Counties. The model would be that of the Swiss cantons, which regard rail transport in their territory as something for which they have a real responsibility to their inhabitants. In the Swiss context there are a large number of private railway companies, party owned or subsidised by the local authorities.

By and large, a tour around the frontiers of privatisation must lead to the conclusion that, while practicable on a scale probably greater than many people have realised, it is fundamentally irrelevant to the long-term problems of the railway industry; and the most alarming aspect is the fear that a Labour Government might seek once again to reverse the process and renationalise the denationalised. This sort of pull-devil, pull-baker does no good to anyone in the long term.

10

The Electrifying Experience

No one can dissent from the argument that electric traction provides the best kind of rail service – clean, fast, and reliable, with substantial cost savings in maintenance and fuel consumption compared with diesel traction. Virtually its only disadvantages are the substantial capital outlay, and the disturbance to existing services during the changeover period. BR has accordingly pressed the case for electrification in paper after paper. From 1978 to 1980 a Steering Group of the Department of Transport and the BRB worked away producing a range of options in which financial analyses were made using computer models to work out effects upon revenues, costs, and return on the investment. The four options which emerged ranged from electrifying a further 23 per cent of the present total network of around 10,500 route miles to electrifying a further 52 per cent and thereby raising the percentage of passenger train miles electrically hauled from the present 40 per cent to an ultimate 83 per cent.

An interesting feature of these options is the 'knock-on' effect; quite simply, the more miles converted and the higher the proportion of the system that is electrified, the better the financial returns. The completed 1980 study gave a net internal rate of return of 11.1 per cent on the largest option (5,750 route miles) and rather similar results for the intermediate options, but only 9.9 per cent on the smallest option (2,580 route miles). The options can also be expressed rather differently. Taking the period of work as lasting 15 years (incidentally, also that adopted in the 1955 Modernisation Plan, which contemplated much more electrification than has actually been carried out) the fastest rate of working would enable the highest mileage to be converted, while the slowest would only achieve the lowest.

BR has two powerful arguments. One is the environmental advantage, as well as the macro-economic desirability of reducing consumption of oil fuel (North Sea supplies having a limited life). Another is the financial justification, which is based less upon improved revenue from more attractive BR services than upon reduced maintenance and operating costs. Underlying these arguments is the need for an uninterrupted or 'rolling' programme, if costs are to be minimised. The planning teams must have a steady work-load, otherwise from time to time they will be disbanded and can only slowly and laboriously be re-recruited and trained for the resumption of work; similarly, manufacturers need forward contracts to ensure continuity in production runs on an economic basis.

What has held back recent Governments so long from accepting the sort of commitment with which a Conservative Government launched the Modernisation Plan of 1955? Despite a few defects and miscalculations, that Plan effectively transformed and modernised BR's services in only 15 years. Two reasons can be suggested. One is the reluctance to make investment in the public sector, which seems to affect Conservative Governments as an article of pure dogma. The second is scepticism about the soundness of the estimated financial returns (despite the magic of computer modelling).

Most of the approvals given recently to relatively minor schemes such as Tonbridge–Hastings, Bishop's Stortford–Cambridge, and Colchester–Norwich are essentially for infilling; they are extensions of existing electrifications which should never have been so curtailed as to involve so much 'synergy', or dual traction, with diesels running under the wire, or over the third rail, an inherently uneconomic and anomalous practice. Perhaps pressure could now reasonably be exerted to get rid of some other anomalies, bits of non-electrified track joining otherwise electrified areas. Some which immediately suggest themselves included Edinburgh–Glasgow (47 miles), Liverpool–Manchester (30 miles), Preston–Blackpool (29 miles by two routes) and Manchester–Leeds (43 miles). There are also small nonsenses such as omitting Royston–Cambridge and Cambridge–King's Lynn from present schemes under implementation, still involving changes in traction or break of journey on through routes, which are inherently uneconomic and inconvenient.

There are, in particular, gaps in the Southern Region's otherwise comprehensive electrified network which need infilling: Portsmouth (Cosham) to Southampton (St Denys), (18 miles), Bournemouth to Weymouth (35 miles), South Croydon to Uckfield and East Grinstead (43 miles), Ash Junction to Wokingham, and Guildford to Tonbridge (51 miles). The latter would greatly improve the Gatwick Airport rail links. None of these straightforward third-rail extensions would raise difficult planning problems or interference during the changeover with existing services; all would improve service quality and reduce maintenance costs.

When one comes to consider complete new main line projects, above all the East Coast Main Line from London to Edinburgh, approved in July 1984, major policy questions emerge. It may be recalled that BR did for a time toy with the idea of basing all Anglo-Scottish services upon the West Coast route, with a Carstairs/Edinburgh link (28 miles only needing to be electrified), and reducing Newcastle–Edinburgh to a single-track with only a skeleton train service. But this has now been buried for good, no doubt much to the relief of Dundee and Aberdeen, as well as of Edinburgh.

There is a certain 'knock-on' effect in the ECML project insofar as the main line is already electrified to Hitchin, and the worst 32 miles (London terminus and the congested suburban area with multiple tracks, station reconstructions and no fewer than seven tunnels) have been dealt with already. But, if one asks how far the passenger will experience better service, ten years ago this question could have been answered more easily than today. The relatively new 100 mph electric Inter-City trains from Euston had then set a new standard of speed and comfort compared with diesel locomotive-hauled trains elsewhere. But the advent of the IC125 sets has made a great difference. Their service speed is higher than that of the LMR electrics despite the upgrading (here and there) to 110 mph over the West Coast line, and the Mark III coaches offer a comparable ride in HST and locomotive-hauled formations.

Where then is the real advantage here? Savings in East Coast journey times will not be substantial. The gain chiefly accrues to the operators, with a more reliable form of traction, simpler, easier and cheaper to maintain. In addition, the environmental and fuel policy advantages (not immediately apparent to the passenger) will be significant in the long term. It is cost savings rather than revenue creation that have won the day.

The Midland main line (Bedford to Sheffield) is an electrification scheme that also would be facilitated by the work already done in electrifying the most congested and costly section, the London area. Just under 50 miles of the main line are now 'under the wires'. This would also be a conveniently self-contained project so far as the principal passenger services are concerned – more so in fact than the East Coast Main Line.

Can the North-East/South-West cross-country route stand on its own, or would it not depend upon the Midland scheme as well as the East Coast? With both completed, NE-SW would slip neatly into place as largely 'infilling', except of course for a big question-mark hanging over the route south of Birmingham. In many of its features – gradients, junctions, speed restrictions and the need for fairly frequent stops – the line is a strong candidate for electrification. The improved acceleration and reliability that the 'juice' offers would further improve on what has already been achieved through the allocation of IC125s to this formerly rather dismal (from the train performance aspect) route, together of course with economies in operating cost.

Lastly, what about the Western Region? For years the Great Western Railway stoutly rejected electrification, although it did commission a report on a Taunton–Penzance scheme, selected on account of the heavy gradients; outside observers commented that if the GWR had been serious, it would have been the main line to South Wales that should have been studied. Now indeed that is the route that is included in the 'high option', all 191 miles from Paddington to Swansea.

Is this a serious proposition? A major difficulty is the spread of Western Region routes, like fingers of a hand. Electrification to South Wales would no doubt embrace Bath, Bristol and Weston-super-Mare. But the main West of England services (even if limited to the old main line via Bristol), the Oxford to Worcester line, the Gloucester and Cheltenham branch, not to mention the Welsh routes – all these cannot easily be 'integrated' into an electrified network. Much dual traction and probably also change of trains for passengers would be involved.

And the Western Region has set particularly high standards with its IC125 network, even though the fleet has been plundered to enable the Midland line to get a long overdue HST service. Exchanges between an electrified Western and the other Regions would involve electrification between Birmingham and Bristol on the NE/SW route, and south-west of Bristol if large diesel mileages 'under the wire' were to be avoided. And what about the inter-Regional services from Manchester, Liverpool and Birmingham to Southern England, either via the West London line or via Reading–Guildford?

There are several major issues. First, a decision on really large-scale electrification following the East Coast Main Line must depend on Government committing itself to (a) an expression of faith in BR's future as a major carrier; (b) environmental factors; (c) the arguments about the future fuel cost balance as between oil and electricity; (d) assisting employment and profitability in a wide range of supporting supply industries; and (e) giving the trades unions confidence in the Government's intention to support the national railway system to an extent that will encourage them to co-operate in more productivity measures. The deal struck (belatedly) over single-manning on the Midland electric trains should and could become the prototype of many more, if a better future for the industry, largely based upon electrification, is to be envisaged.

There must in any case be strong justification for the infillings based upon existing electrifications mentioned above, together with a second main line project rolling behind the East Coast scheme. The strongest candidate is probably the Midland line, Bedford to Sheffield via Derby and via Nottingham, largely because of its compact, self-contained character. If the North East–South West route were to follow, the programme would really roll and the unit costs of the total package would be minimised.

11

The Freight Factor

If one received impressions of BR solely from the media, one might be excused for assuming that it was exclusively a passenger railway. Passengers are news; freight is not, save perhaps when there is a hullaballoo over the transport by rail of nuclear waste – surely much more safely and unobtrusively than by road? Yet, it is not so long since freight receipts outweighed those from passengers. In the first year after nationalisation, for instance, rail traffic receipts were divided in the proportions of 63.3 per cent from freight and parcels, 36.7 per cent from passengers. Today the tables are almost exactly reversed: in 1983 only 35.8 per cent from freight and parcels, but 64.2 per cent from passenger fares etc. If Government support for the passenger business is included then the comparison is even more striking: only 23.4 per cent from freight, against 76.6 per cent from passengers. In 1948 309 million tonnes of freight were carried: in 1983 only 145 millions. Even so, freight remains a very considerable business.

The British Road Federation estimates that the railways carry about 10 per cent of the tonnage handled by road, and about 16 per cent of the tonne-kilometres achieved by road. But that is not really a valid comparison of the market share; there has always been an important part of the national total which is reserved to road from its nature – local delivery work for instance. It is the rail's share of the traffic that could pass either by road or rail that is significant, and here the rail proportion is very much higher.

However, there is no denying that the fall in the tonnage carried by rail, almost continuous over the past 30 years or so, has created the most acute of BR's financial problems. Even though traffic costing was in 1948 an even more approximate

Steam buffs sometimes forget just how polluting steam could be *(Derek Cross)*

The London Midland main line electrification has paid off handsomely; why had it no successor until the East Coast main line scheme was approved in 1984? *(British Rail)*

Whitemoor Up Yard control tower, in the days when wagonload freight was still overwhelmingly predominant *(British Rail)*

Today merry-go-round trainload business dominates *(British Rail)*

science (or, rather, art) than it is today, it has long been held that freight is the more profitable side of the business. The present Government insists that the Freight Sector should be at least self-supporting and BR accepts the commitment.

An important aspect of the freight business is its interaction with the passenger side. For instance, the West Coast Main Line electrification enables locomotives to work passenger trains by day and freight by night, whereas the East Coast Main Line's IC125 diesel sets today provide no traction for freight trains when the passenger service is inoperative.

Another aspect of passenger and freight traffic interdependence is the occasional need to keep sections of line open on a three-shift basis to cover freight and parcels (mainly newspaper and mails) at night, whereas passenger service may only require two-shift working. However, in the rather artificial world of separate costings for the Sectors in BR, the concept of prime user generally works to the advantage of the Freight Sector, since the majority of freight moves over routes more heavily occupied by Inter-City or Provincial trains. This means that the Sector is only debited with those costs estimated to be 'escapable' if the freight service were withdrawn. The boot can of course be on the other foot, where a heavy freight line also carries some passenger traffic but is charged as prime user. It is all very arbitrary and sometimes capricious in its effects.

How does one explain the fact that freight tonnage is so much less than it was at the time of nationalisation? Four main reasons appear. The first is the change in Britain's industrial structure since 1948; the relative decline in the basic industries traditionally relying on rail transport has been matched by the rise of secondary and service industries relying mainly if not exclusively upon road transport. Secondly, there has been a passive acceptance by successive Governments of the build-up of commercial road transport, even up to the point at which much of the road system is unable to cope with it properly. Deregulation and competition seem to have been considered to promote economic growth; the earlier scrapping of the licensing system for road haulage vehicles (followed by that for long-distance coaches) sometimes appears like a belated echo of the Conservative Party's 'Set the People Free' slogan of the 1951 Election campaign. 'Making a bonfire of controls' may have been a refreshing approach at the end of post-war austerity and rationing; its renewal at a time not of expansion but of recession was not particularly well timed. If rising Government expenditure on the road system were available to match the increase in weight and number of heavy vehicles using the highways there might have been more justification for this transport philosophy. In fact, it did not match the policy of restricting public sector investment.

A third major cause of the decline in rail freight was the Beeching 'Re-Shaping'. Commercially, the effect of the publicity given to that document was disastrous. Traders looked at the list of stations and lines which were possible candidates for closure (many of which remain open today) and too often made arrangements to transfer their traffic to road. A few years earlier the Eastern Region's Planning Office had produced a map entitled, 'The Economic Eastern Region', indicating those lines which might not survive a costing exercise. The Area Board Chairman, Sir Reginald Wilson, having examined the map with keen interest, directed that it should be kept under lock and key lest traders should assume that it would lead to early closures and take precautions accordingly. He was in this respect better advised than Dr Beeching later on, though in fairness to the Doctor one must appreciate that Beeching was expected to show some results, and very quickly, by his political sponsors. The 'Re-shaping' however under-estimated the knock-on effect of closures and the reaction upon the economics of the freight business of a decline in volume in face of relatively inflexible costs. For instance, cutting out uneconomic terminals may mean that other terminals remaining in operation, hitherto economic, may lose so much traffic that they themselves become uneconomic. This downward spiral was not fully understood or evaluated.

Fourthly, there were some miscalculations by BR itself around the period of the 1955 Modernisation Plan. The assumptions regarding the future of wagon-load freight were too optimistic; they led to the new marshalling yard programme and such white elephants as the Bletchley flyover. On the other hand, the Plan was undoubtedly right in stressing the importance of eliminating the loose-coupled hand-braked wagon as quickly as possible. Unfortunately, the choice of the vacuum brake instead of the compressed-air brake was a major factor in holding up the achievement of this important objective. It has taken 30 years since the launch of the Modernisation Plan freight train virtually to eliminate from BR the loose-coupled freight train, devoid of continuous power brakes.

This delay has greatly hampered the freight business in competing with road, by limiting its ability to offer quick and reliable service. There were of course other factors at work, but it is rather ironic that BR is now very well equipped to handle much freight that has been lost to roads, by providing air-braked Speedlink wagons, fast train times and information from the TOPS computer, which might have ensured the retention of the traffic had these facilities existed in the 1950s and 1960s.

Early in 1984 one would have said that the BR freight strategy appeared to be well devised, with a good prospect of reaching the Government's financial target. After nearly a year of the coal strike, unfortunately, it was in some disarray, through no fault of the railways. It was particularly tragic that, with two-thirds of the mines not producing coal, some drivers in the Midlands where the pits were working refused to handle coal trains so that road hauliers gleefully seized the opportunity to invade a traffic that had always seemed secure for the railways.

Disregarding the coal strike, the long-term prospects can be divided into traffic groups. First, the train-load business. Here, the short average length of haul in Britain (73.4 miles in 1983) is an adverse factor. Another is the decline in those industries – coal and steel – embraced in Sir Peter Parker's epigram that 'BR is basic to the basic industries'. Just how basic are they still, in view of the long-term changes in Britain's economic structure, the growth of substitute fuels and substitute materials for industry? The growth in merry-go-round coal trains, from only 35 trains a day to over 200, and the more than doubling the tonnage of trainload traffic between the mid-1960s and the later 1970s was excellent. But there it seems to have stuck. Where are the expanding markets for train-load? Not coal or steel, presumably, but other bulk goods which now move by road, especially in tankers, may be fields for exploration. In this connection one cannot overlook the alarming consequences of road accidents arising from lorries jack-knifing on motorways and elsewhere when carrying oil or dangerous chemicals. Encouraging all such traffic to change to rail would be a worthwhile exercise for any Government that cares about safety and the environment.

Of course the logical development lies in the Freightliner concept, in theory the most rational way of using both road and rail to assist in the 'container revolution'. Why then has Freightliner crept rather than leapt ahead since it was launched in the 1960s as the answer to modern freight transport needs?

One answer may be the rather arms-length relationship established with the railways when the business was placed under the National Freight Corporation. Another may be the absence of any Government policy to assist traffic to transfer to Freightliner by adjusting taxation on a more realistic basis against the heavy road container vehicle – in effect continuing to subsidise the use of motorways by HGV's, through taxes levied on the private motorist.

Containerisation has grown most dramatically in import and export traffic. But development within the Continental counterpart to Freightliner, the Inter-Container Company, has been disappointingly slow, partly owing to the European railways' adherence to wagon-load systems rather than the Freightliner trainload concept. Had the Channel Tunnel not been cancelled in 1975, but instead opened in 1981, the international container business with British Rail would look very different today, with great environmental as well as financial gains to the economy. The Harold Wilson Government bears a heavy responsibility for cancelling the Tunnel just as many years of laborious preparation had been brought to a conclusion and work on the actual boring was on the point of starting.

Many motorists, held up by a juggernaut belching exhaust fumes, have muttered 'That load ought to be on the railway'. The stock counter-argument from the road side is that the railway does not run to the house or shop, or even very often nowadays into the factory. Consequently, roads have to be used at each end of the trunk haul for collection and delivery. So where, it is asked, is the gain? Furthermore, the road interests argue that since road-rail transits involve the use of road transport for making up or breaking down trainloads into smaller road vehicles, more lorries in total are needed than if the large trunk-haul vehicle performs the entire job.

This argument does not deal with the point that some of our motorways and bridges are coming close to collapse under the weight of HGV traffic. And the heavy goods vehicle has been shown by the Government's own Transport & Road Research Laboratory to be subsidised by the taxpayer, in that its tax payments come nowhere near to meeting the costs of damage that it causes to the road system.

Two measures therefore could be considered. One would be a substantial and long overdue readjustment of the rates of taxation on the effectively subsidised HGVs; another to follow the example of France, Italy and, since the beginning of 1985, Switzerland, and levy tolls for the use of the motorways, above all by HGVs, which might provide the finance to put them and maintain them (even perhaps the infamous Spaghetti Junction!) in proper repair.

A further measure would be the extension of Section 8 grants (the grants for rail connections to industrial establishments which do not possess them) for the construction of more Freightliner terminals for road/rail interchange. The heavy capital cost of the equipment for rapid road-rail transfer has been a factor inhibiting the growth of Freightliner which is, in principle, the best system for relieving the main roads of miscellaneous freight and yet providing door-to-door container delivery services.

Train-load or wagon-load? The doctrine of 'train-load only' that emerged in the 1960s may have thrown the baby out with the bath-water. Can the Speedlink concept of timetabled through trains between major centres be adapted to the relatively small volume of internal British trade that moves in trainloads, other than bulk materials and liquids? BR long ago lost most of the trainload business in perishables – the Aberdeen fish, the Avonmouth banana specials, the Cornish broccoli expresses, the West Country milk trains. But what about groupage traffic by Speedlink, for sundries to be collected and delivered by National Carriers Ltd? After all, historically road and rail have always been partners. The construction of the railways, although it killed the stage-coach and the lumbering long-distance horse-drawn wagon, actually increased the volume of road traffic. 'The horse-drawn road traffic of the country ... grew steadily through the early railway age. The railways were fed, in the jingle of the nursery, by "coach, carriage, wheelbarrow, cart." '*

Pickfords in the early days worked in close association with the railway, not merely as cartage agents but as carriers dealing with the public and employing the railway for trunk hauls; the firm for some time even managed the Camden Goods Depot of the London & Birmingham Railway – now a depot of National Carriers Ltd, the wheel having come full circle! The breaking down of road/rail links under successive Transport Acts has created an artificial opposition between two forms of transport that are really more complementary than competitive. In particular, the 1968 Transport Act, excellent in many ways, went wrong in its attempt to foster road-rail co-ordination. It was right to promote the creation of National Carriers Ltd as an amalgam of BR's collection and delivery services and BRS (Parcels) and it was also correct to give it BR's Sundries business, including ownership of the associated rail terminals. But it was wrong to place NCL under the National Freight Corporation, which was wholly road-orientated. National Carriers enjoyed the benefit of effective management and many reforms were instituted; but the pious injunction in the Transport Act 1968 to use rail whenever this was 'efficient and economic' (those sacred cows of the civil service) was quietly ignored. The advantages of a combined road and rail sundries network would much more probably have been obtained had NCL been a BR subsidiary.

In Holland a better prototype existed for many years in the firm of Van Gend & Loos, a distribution and road transport subsidiary of the Netherlands Railways; it is a great pity that this example was not followed here. Of course, BR, harassed over its deficit in the late 1960s, was not sorry at the time to see its loss-making sundries and road cartage activities taken over by someone else; in the long run, though, NCL should, like Van Gend & Loos, have been motivated to use rail for longer transits

---

* Sir John Clapham, *Economic History of Modern Britain*, I, p. 403

and groupage traffic. It is not too late to correct this imbalance especially now that Speedlink can provide NCL with just the kind of fast and reliable service the traffic requires, with airbraked wagons that can run at 75mph, and an information system in TOPS that can rectify the uncertainty and slowness that used to characterise some of the nation-wide freight service that BR formerly offered.

Can a general wagon-load business survive within the Speedlink concept? Today, wagon-load is barely one-fifth of train-load business, and some argue that it should disappear altogether. Speedlink in fact adopts a pragmatic attitude. In theory, individual wagons are not collected for assembly into trainloads, but in practice small rakes will be collected, much depending on the type of traffic and the importance of the trader's business in total. It can be suggested that trip working may not be uneconomic if, for instance, the trip locomotive is a diesel shunter and single-manned. (Problems such as line occupation by relatively slow-moving units and the responsibility for coupling and uncoupling should scarcely present insoluble difficulties.)

If trip working is not ruled out, the inducement for traders to apply for Section 8 grants will be increased. Even Freightliners, the arch-priests of trainload, have looked at the scope for assembling and breaking down trainloads – one recalls PUFF (Programme for the Utilisation of Fractional Freightliners)!

The other headache is road-rail transhipment; must this be concentrated upon Freightliner terminals, with their heavy capital costs? So far, no one has yet come up with a completely satisfactory Road-rail vehicle, despite many experimental ventures. However, today there are several designs of mobile or semi-mobile container transfer systems in existence and one at least in Britain has been under test with financial support from the Department of Transport for its development as a research project.

If the Government is sincere in its expression of pious hope for a transfer of traffic from road to rail – good for the environment, good for the Treasury which pays for the motorways, good for BR – how can firms that have invested considerable sums in their heavy goods vehicles, especially tankers, be persuaded to change to rail? In view of the social costs by HGVs, far exceeding their taxation contributions, it would make sense for any Government to adopt fiscal measures designed to persuade traders not to replace their HGVs when due for renewal but to consider rail transport, either through obtaining a Section 8 grant of 60 per cent of the cost of a rail connection to their premises, or (where such connection is not feasible), assistance towards the purchase of any practicable design of road-rail vehicle, either tanker or container type.

As a final comment, while the difficulties of the post-nationalisation period have from time to time been exacerbated by one or two miscalculations on the part of the railways themselves, today's BR freight strategy seems to be correct, if only it can be pushed hard enough. But successive Governments must bear some responsibility for the unbalanced and uneconomic division of traffic and utilisation of resources as between road and rail. Thus, in addition to a vigorous policy of self-help by BR, some positive steps by Government would be fully justified, not as an act of charity towards BR but in the national interest. One or two ways in which this could be exercised have been suggested; there may well be others.

12

Tomorrow's Railpersons and the
Role of the Unions

This chapter started life as 'Tomorrow's Railwaymen', but since it contains a plea for the wider employment of women within BR, the more cumbersome expression has perforce been adopted, since 'man' no longer embraces 'woman', as used to be the case! There is an obvious point, that a service industry in direct contact with its public depends more upon the attitude to the job of its staff than upon any other single factor. Efficient, helpful staff can provide an acceptable level of service even where equipment is old-fashioned, provided it has been kept in tip-top condition, clean and in full repair. In contrast, unhelpful or scruffy staff can ruin the impact of shiny new trains and rebuilt stations. Yet formerly the recruitment and training of staff did not receive a very high degree of top management's attention. Of course, between the wars even the basic features of personnel work – negotiation on wages and conditions – demanded less attention than they do today, because there was no annual round of pay talks and crises such as the General Strike of 1926 were few and far between. 'Staff' work was sometimes therefore regarded as a specialist area into which those unlikely to reach top operating or commercial posts could conveniently be shunted. There were notable exceptions – men such as Kenelm Kerr of the LNER were no mean administrators – but lower down the line there was sometimes a rather bureaucratic outlook, matched now and again by some on the trade union side who enjoyed legalistic arguments and hairsplitting.

In recent years this has been changed, largely by drafting more of the ablest managers into personnel work, not always perhaps at their own wish. One need only mention Alex Dunbar, John Roberts, Charles McLeod and Cliff Rose in this connection. And imported talent in the person of (Sir) Leonard Neal made a considerable impact. Sometimes an imaginative approach from the management side – as in the case of the 'Windsor' and 'Penzance' agreements on productivity – could produce a response from the other side and lead to real progress. But thereafter the haggling over details of implementation has been too prone to reappear, with depressing results.

What sort of staff does BR need today, to present a really convincing new image to the public, to Parliament and the media? It is important to shed any impression of stuffiness, or of bureaucratic procedures, that could give the lie to the bright promises of television advertising; 'The Age of the Train' had begun to look middle-aged before it was dropped.

An obvious move is to stimulate the recruitment of women – young, intelligent and attractive – into booking offices, enquiry offices, ticket checking, restaurant and buffet cars, in fact wherever the railway's competitors such as airlines and coaches employ women. If the answer is that this is already being done, then one can only say that the 'staff men', although they have recruited some very suitable girls, have also taken on some whom the airlines and coach companies would have turned down. A good personality, the ability to speak pleasantly, clearly and distinctly – even in regional accents – and looking good in a smart uniform are absolutely essential; with the protection of employment legislation now in force, a mistake in recruiting an individual may be impossible to rectify later. This does of course pre-suppose that the staff people responsible for recruitment have the ability to pick out the right applicants.

One airline recruits its stewardesses thus. First comes a day of interviews and written tests. Those who succeed are invited to the second stage, a month later – a whole day devoted to psychological testing, followed by a very thorough medical check on the following day. The survivors are then posted to a training course lasting several weeks during which their response to training is critically observed and some further weeding-out is applied before firm engagements are offered; and even then, the first three months are a probationary period.

No one would consider quite such rigorous procedures necessary for railway work although comprehensive training would be needed in railway geography, train services and facilities and fares and charges, for ticket and enquiry office recruits; nor is the flood of applicants as large as that for airline work. But some more systematic and selective procedures could well be applied; the easier it is to enter a job, the less impressive the standard of applicants is likely to be – and it is not simply a matter of money. Railway work involves variety and often change of scene, and valuable travel privileges; its attractions should be better exploited. Training in some areas could well be more positive; in the past too much reliance has been placed on putting a raw recruit in the company of experienced men – good as far as it goes but the newcomers tend to pick up any bad procedures and short cuts which have become established by tradition.

The unions are not usually enthusiastic about the recruitment of women, though remaining male chauvinism is becoming muted. Too much has been made of the problems associated with employment of women, and too little of the advantages – attention to appearances and cleanliness, helpfulness towards the elderly or very young, greater conscientiousness in carrying out routine tasks, for example.

Apart from the need for a better balance between the sexes in railway work, what impression does one have of today's railwayman? How far do traditional practices survive, and do they hinder BR from emerging from twilight into sunshine? What sort of railperson will be needed in the 21st century? (It is only a decade and a half away.)

Before the second world war, work on the railways was considered desirable, to the extent that there was seldom any difficulty in recruitment. It was not highly paid by, for example, the standards of the steel or textile industries. Much of the work was arduous; firing and driving a steam locomotive are physically taxing duties as well as demanding considerable skills. Work on the track involved (as it still does) hard manual labour in all weathers. But railways offered security, a wide range of tasks providing interest and some job satisfaction, the ladders of promotion based principally upon seniority. In consequence, it was usually possible to pick and choose among applicants for vacancies. In country areas, the railway wage of a shilling or two above the agricultural labourer's rate was sufficient inducement for men to leave the land. Recruitment still retained slight traces of the early railway practice of directors personally interviewing or recommending all applicants, since vacancies were often filled through stationmasters' and other supervisors' personal knowledge of suitable youngsters to fill starting grade posts, and women typists and clerks were often daughters or sisters of railwaymen.

This system had two results. First, it attracted, on the whole, steady, reliable workers into the railways – a point of prime importance in a service industry. Second, it promoted a strong 'family' feeling amongst railwaymen akin to, if not quite as strong as that in the armed services, with which the railways have always had some affinity. Their managers were 'officers', their luncheon rooms 'messes'. The rule book was the equivalent of King's Regulations. Discipline, originally based on safety considerations in the days when signalling was primitive and slight human errors could easily cause disasters, was strict, with punishments and commendations recorded on every employee's history sheet.

Of course, among a labour force of over 600,000, a few black sheep were bound to exist, but on the whole the popular image of the railwayman as a decent, conscientious worker was well justified.

During the second world war, railwaymen were in general a reserved occupation, though a number volunteered for military service and eventually younger men were called up. The work of those who carried on has been rightly praised for it was often dangerous as well as arduous. But the need to keep the railways running at all costs meant that management felt unable to insist upon pre-war disciplinary standards and the few black sheep did not have to watch their conduct so closely.

After the war things became difficult. There was disillusionment with the results of nationalisation, since wages and conditions changed far less than people had been led to hope. The hidden hand of the British Transport Commission – and, behind the BTC, the Government – was felt when early demands for wage increases were declined by the Railway

Executive. Clerks who had been colonels and squadron leaders were not always happy to return to their pre-war status. At the same time, the weakening of managerial authority, at supervisory level in particular, created by the need to avoid disputes at local level and keep the job going, continued; it was now exacerbated by the difficulty of recruitment in an era of full (or over-full) employment. Railway wages failed for a time to keep pace with the general advance; in consequence, recruitment difficulties had sometimes to be solved by accepting unsuitable applicants who before the war would have been turned away. Older railwaymen often regarded them with dismay.

With the gradual improvement in railway pay scales that began with the Guillebaud report on 'comparability' (with other industries) of 1958, and the first break-through in negotiations with the unions on productivity, namely the Penzance and Windsor agreements of 1968, the recruitment position improved. The recession that began in 1973 made railway work relatively more attractive. The Youth Opportunities Scheme has also brought into the railways a number of youngsters, some of whom have proved to be well worth recruiting to the permanent staff.

Today's railwaymen are therefore a mixed lot. There is a leavening of older men of the traditional, responsible type – good railwaymen in every sense. There are many promising younger men also. In between come some excellent people, but also some whose attitude to railway work is not all that it should be, who were all that could be taken on in the big cities in the days of over-full employment. They will not leave, now that the economic climate has turned colder, and when railway pay and conditions are relatively much more attractive than when they were originally recruited.

It is curious that morale can sometimes be low and readiness to take some form of industrial action high among just those grades whose working conditions have improved most markedly in the past 25 years – drivers, secondmen (driver's assistants – call them what you will) – and guards. Compare the work of a modern diesel or electric locoman, or a dmu or emu driver, with that of his steam predecessor; he now has all-weather protection, an excellent view ahead, warmth and a

153

seated position, simple controls – all facilities formerly lacking. Historians have laughed at the early locomotive superintendents who refused to design cabs giving footplatemen full weather protection, on the grounds that if they were made too comfortable, their vigilance would suffer. (A similar argument was long used by Scotland Yard to justify the refusal to permit all-weather cabs to be provided for London tram, bus, and taxi drivers.) But perhaps there is after all some connection between the difficulty of a job and the morale of the worker? Even so, of course, no one would contemplate a return to the practices of the last century. Yet lax supervision leads to practices that are hard to defend. A minor case in point is the observance of 'whistle' signs at automatic half-barrier level crossings. The Chief Inspecting Officer of Railways, in approving the design, required the provision of two 'whistle' boards on each side approaching the new crossings. 'W' signs accordingly are provided; but any regular traveller who is familiar with railway working knows that they are obeyed or disregarded (chiefly the latter) entirely at the whim of individual drivers. Now, *either* the boards are essential on safety grounds, in which case drivers should be disciplined for failing to observe them; *or* they are unnecessary, in which case management should ask the Inspecting Officer to agree to their removal. The present situation, in which drivers are allowed to ignore an order imposed, rightly or wrongly, on safety grounds, is illogical.

It is true that drivers in Britain have traditionally been given more individual discretion than is common in most other countries. Some men will 'run hard' to overtake any lateness caused by factors outside their control; others seem to become defeatist and allow lateness to continue or even increase. Management for years presented drivers with an excuse for irregular running, by failing to provide them with official timepieces – something that has now been rectified. The meticulous care with which a Swiss driver will observe his passing times, checking them against the working timetable, clipped open at the appopriate page on the control console, stands out against the more easy-going British practice where drivers memorise or jot down their timings on odd pieces of paper. Moreover the Swiss drivers' timetable book is designed for *his* use and includes permanent speed restrictions, unlike British working timetables, which are for all operating staff.

There is also a question of status. A top-link express passenger steam driver used to be very conscious of being a master craftsman, respected by his juniors in the motive power depot. Driving an IC125 today does not carry quite the same prestige, despite the achievement of very high speeds. And on the Southern, a man may be on a fast Bournemouth run one week and down the Waterloo & City tube the next. The pay packet is important as ever but status differentials have become of less significance.

Curiously enough station staff, whose working conditions have not been eased very significantly by comparison with those of, say, drivers, seem less prone to militancy than are the train crews. The same seems to apply to civil engineering staff, especially permanent way men. Their work, despite mechanisation of many operations, still involves much hard physical labour and exposure to all sorts of weather. One unpleasant duty has almost disappeared – that of acting as fog-signalman. Its cold and boring nature used to be only partly compensated by enhanced earnings. These grades, incidentally, originally accepted work study as leading to greater productivity, much more easily than their colleagues on the trains accepted flexible rostering.

The goods guard of former days had an arduous job. Acting as brakesman for a heavy loose-coupled freight train called for skill and experience; he also kept an eye open for wagon defects on the move. Today's BR goods guard mostly rides in the locomotive as a second man, in comparative comfort; his duties are minimal. In Denmark every freight train dispenses with a guard; in Switzerland a single-manned locomotive will take a heavy freight train right across the country from the German frontier at Basel to the Italian frontier at Chiasso without a guard. Safety is not in question; Swiss drivers are in radio contact with signalboxes and (as on BR where modern centralised signalling has been installed), hot axlebox detectors on the lineside provide surveillance against this type of defect. So is there any long-term need for a second man on British freight trains?

Where passenger guards are still, and will continue to be

needed, as on main line trains, surely they should be required not merely to perform station duties but, as well as checking passengers' tickets, to patrol the train frequently, assisting passenger comfort, regulating the heating if necessary, closing windows that are causing draughts and heat loss in winter, observing missing light bulbs and replacing them without waiting for complaints from passengers, and discouraging, simply by their frequent presence, vandalism or bad behaviour. They should, as was formerly the case, enjoy authority and be prepared to exercise it. This applies especially to the need to wear uniform at all times; passengers have on occasions been asked to produce their tickets by a conductor-guard wearing ordinary clothes. How could this man in an emergency expect to exert authority over passengers, for instance ordering them to leave or not to leave a train stopped out of course, or involved in an incident? It is essential that staff in contact with the public are always supplied with, and required to wear, all the uniform that indicates their status and authority. Failure to supply in good time a well-fitting uniform can sometimes be an administrative failure calling for investigation and rectification.

Local management has sometimes been lax in this matter; equally, a few individuals seem to take delight in replacing part of their uniform with often eccentric items of clothing. They seem oblivious to the effect upon BR's image that scruffiness produces.

'Productivity' is today the main issue dividing BR's management and the unions, but better industrial discipline is just as important. There must be a mixture of firmness and commonsense, knowing when to stand fast and when to concede a point. If supervisors are over-ruled by higher management, they will of course lose interest in maintaining standards. Lastly, it is not just managerial support for supervisors that is essential but also procedures for selecting them dominated more by suitability and less by seniority than in the past.

Returning to productivity, this is an elusive concept in many areas of railway work, where attendance is required but the pace of work is determined by its character rather than by the motivation of the employee. Signalmens' duties are an obvious

Safer on the rail: a train of anhydrous ammonia tanks from Teesside to Scotland *(Ian S. Carr)*

At the heart of the Freightliner concept, the very costly road-rail transfer equipment *(British Rail)*

Concern for the heritage: King's Cross, originally a fine, bold and simple concept, had been ruined by the clutter in front . . . *(British Rail)* . . . but now, unlike Euston, combines new facilities with the best of the original design *(Author)*

example. But there is scope for much improvement in the application of agreements at local level; flexible rostering is a good example. Conceded in principle at national level, there is a danger that an agreement will not be applied energetically by supervisors anxious to avoid disputes. This is of course also the history of single-manning on locomotives, conceded in principle as long ago as the late 1960s and still only patchily in force. There is really no case for a second man on any diesel or electric locomotive except where he is under training, performing shunter's duties, or working locomotives with the old style train heating boilers. The need for a second man on IC125s is certainly questionable. High speed inevitably demands full concentration, but the presence of a second man in the cab can lead to conversation and loss of concentration; the deadman's vigilance pedal or handle, and existence of aws, are adequate protection in the event of a driver's sudden illness or forgetfulness.

What of tomorrow's railwaymen? One cannot change human nature in the case of a small minority whose attitude to the job is unsuitable. BR is already paying more attention to the training or retraining of staff in contact with the public, in the so-called 'charm schools'. Even the driver nowadays may come into this category; traditionally isolated from passengers, the introduction of one-man operation (DOO, OMO or OPO!) on suburban trains has often changed his role. Through the public address system he now has to keep his passengers informed; it is he, no longer the guard, who is formally in charge of the train, and the local representative of BR. Many drivers (like the train operators on the London Underground Ltd Victoria Line) have accepted this role well. But there are still a few (such as those who unnecessarily pull down the blinds behind the driving compartment of dmus in daytime so as to deprive passengers of a view ahead) who seem to dislike the idea of any contact with the public. This attitude needs re-education.

Gradual improvement in staff performance may depend on the replacement of the tiny minority of unsuitable individuals, no easy matter. Here, voluntary redundancy may be the best way of weeding-out on a selective basis, a task calling for perceptiveness on the part of supervisors and tact in dealing with the unions. The second aim must be to make joint consultation more effective; the courses arranged at a country house in Somerset where both sides formerly met in discussion groups served a useful purpose, and this technique could be expanded. Lastly, recruitment is the key to progressive improvement in the quality of staff attitudes, above all in the case of staff in contact with the public. Selective recruitment allied to universal induction training in the starting grades should become more sophisticated. During the period of overfull employment the railways had to accept (often with misgivings) almost any applicant whom the Labour Exchange or the later Job Centre sent along. Selective recruitment was then not possible, against the pressure to fill vacancies and reduce the excessive overtime being worked by existing staff. But today the labour market is different, and more selective recruitment techniques, followed by much more initial training on an institutional basis, are perfectly practicable.

Money spent upon establishing permanent training schools for all 'blue-collar' traffic grades would be a good investment. Again taking the Swiss example, a comprehensive new training school was opened in 1984 for Federal Railways recruits, and for updating existing staff in procedures. There has on BR in the past been overmuch reliance upon rough-and-ready training on the job where, too often, undesirable attitudes to work could be picked up by a recruit from older men whose morale had deteriorated or perhaps had never been very good. Thorough training, and, above all, watchfulness on the part of local supervisors, is the only remedy. But formal training on an institutional basis within BR has been largely confined to managers and supervisors; despite various vocational training courses there has been nothing like London Regional Transport's standard induction training, for the traffic grades at entry. One must admit that BR has problems arising from its geographical dispersal from which London Regional Transport is free, but it is arguable that in several conurbations the intake is sufficient to justify permanent training schools being instituted to replace the present patchwork of courses.

Turning to tomorrow's managers, it can confidently be expected that the quality and quantity of management talent on BR will continue at a high level. The inherent attraction of the railway industry has always been sufficient to recruit young men of ability, and today also some, though not nearly enough, young women. Ever since nationalisation, British Railways recruited into the traffic apprenticeship training scheme (later renamed the management training scheme) a number of university graduates and promising applicants from the clerical staff. More recently suitable school leavers have been also given special training at regional level. After some years in the service, young managers were eligible for a residential course at the BR School of Transport at Derby, while for middle managers who are potential high-flyers the British Transport Staff College at Woking, Surrey, offered business training of a very superior character. Replacing the former rather haphazard and paternalistic system of career planning on the railways, too, a sophisticated management development programme was inaugurated in the 1960s.

So there should be no serious short-comings in the future managerial field, apart from two question-marks. The first is over the unsettling and demoralising effect of frequent reorganisations, which create uncertainty about personal prospects, and divert attention from the work in hand. The second is the recurrence from time to time of scepticism about the value of training or of financial strain in funding it. One example of the former was the reduction in the duration of the management training scheme and the (temporary) exclusion of women from the scheme. The second is exemplified by the BRB's decision to cease its financial support for the British Transport Staff College. Founded in 1959 by the enthusiasm of General Sir Brian Robertson, the College was designed to serve three distinct purposes; first to provide a forum at which middle managers throughout the British Transport Commission's huge and diversified undertaking could get to know each other during a three months' course, a process of 'cross-fertilisation' between railwaymen, busmen, hauliers, waterway and shipping men; second to improve their knowledge of modern techniques chiefly in transport but also in business in general; and third to create a 'goldfish bowl' in which men of outstanding ability could be identified for accelerated promotion, something badly needed at that time in the absence of planned management development on a formal basis.

These functions were admirably fulfilled by the College. In 1962 however the BTC was abolished by the Transport Act of that year, and the BRB had the opportunity to take over the Staff College for purely railway purposes. But other considerations, largely of finance, prevailed and the College became a separate undertaking financed by some but not all of the successor Boards to the BTC. Thereafter the College became rather more of a general business school, maintaining and enhancing its reputation and being attended by people from a wide range of industries and public services, often unconnected with transport. Eventually the BR link was broken, the College premises were sold and the courses transferred to the Ashridge Management College. It is arguable that a great opportunity was missed in 1962, because the BRB – like most great industrial concerns – needs its own staff college to develop the potential high-flyers in its management structure. The Derby School of Transport, originally built by the LMS in the 1930s, also no longer runs its management courses for younger men who are now instead sent to an outside Business School.

Turning from BR's problems, one must ask what is likely to be the future role of the unions? They have to function within an industry that has suffered severe contraction and thus they face special problems which call for sympathetic appreciation before sweeping judgments are made. The rail unions have a long and respectable history. In the 19th century they reflected the needs of railwaymen for mutual support in the face of severe codes of discipline as much as for muscle-power to improve their wages. The early railways only managed to operate with the primitive signalling and braking systems then in force through strict disciplinary codes aimed at ensuring safety. Individuals were sometimes harshly treated in consequence, and the natural comradeship of railwaymen grew into more formal associations for mutual protection. Superimposed on this came the urge to improve living standards, resisted by boards and managements under pressure to keep down costs. There followed demands for recognition and threats of strike action, leading to the elaborate Railway Conciliation Scheme of 1907 always associated with the name of Lloyd George, but actually drafted in essentials by Sam Fay, then General

Manager of the Great Central Railway. For many years thereafter railway industrial relations were considered to be something of a model for other industries. Apart from the strike in 1919 caused by post-war inflation which had eroded the real value of the wage packet, and the trauma of the 1926 General Strike, the elaborate negotiating machinery with its hierarchy of Central and National Wages Boards, National Tribunal, Sectional Councils and Local Departmental Committees, worked fairly smoothly, especially against a background of stable or falling prices. In fact, in 1928 the railways obtained agreement from the unions for an actual reduction in wages and salaries by 2½ per cent all round, which lasted until 1930.

The railway unions moreover threw up a number of able leaders over the period; in the National Union of Railwaymen there were the Rt Hon J. H. Thomas, John Marchbank, and C. T. Cramp; in the Associated Society of Locomotive Engineers & Firemen, John Bromley; and in the Railway Clerks' Association, A. G. Walkden. They were followed by a later generation of leaders that included (Sir) John Benstead, Jim Campbell and S. F. (Lord) Greene in the NUR, W. P. Allen in the ASLEF, and John Bothwell in the RCA (later renamed the Transport Salaried Staffs' Association–TSSA.).

Today however the weight of the railway unions has declined, in company with that of their partners in the so-called Triple Alliance of railwaymen, the coal miners and the steel workers. Formerly there were good grounds for believing that concerted action by these labour giants could, if necessary, bring the country to its knees. Now the economy can survive, apparently, almost indefinitely if the railways, the mines or the steelworks shut down. Competitors – road transport, oil and North Sea gas, light alloys and plastics, not to mention imports of coal and steel – have cut the ground from under the feet of these former 'basic' industries upon which our economic structure depended. This is a hard pill for the railway unions to swallow, and in some quarters there seems to be an outdated but lingering belief that railways are still essential to national survival.

This is wishful thinking; in fact, every strike, every stoppage proves the opposite. Railways no longer enjoy a birthright; they have to struggle to prove their usefulness, and that they still have a part to play, to any government that has the ear of the strong road lobby.

Yet with the railway unions' great historical significance, and their tradition of producing labour leaders of national stature, it is sad if the general public today receives through the media an impression that the unions are trigger-happy, too ready to support their case by inconveniencing the public and the rail commuter in particular. It does not conform with the traditional image of the railwayman as a responsible, fair-minded public servant. The problem exists however at both local and national level.

At local level, as suggested above, perhaps boredom, the lack of variety or even difficulty in the work, may lead to a drop in morale and a willingness to walk out on any pretext. At national level, the unions may well feel that they are in a critical position. Their membership has been falling year after year, as BR's total staff has declined. This not only affects their income from membership dues but also their relative influence in the trade union movement as a whole. They may (not surprisingly) feel that survival depends upon exerting themselves, upon being seen to fight strenuously not just for the pay packet by also job numbers and union dues. The seriousness of the unions' problem can be illustrated by the drop in membership between 1961 and 1982. The NUR fell by 52.7 per cent, the ASLEF by 52.5 per cent, and the TSSA by 34.5 per cent.

Things are not made easier by the existence of a craft union – ASLEF – alongside the nominally all-embracing NUR as an industrial union, in addition to a separate union (TSSA) for salaried clerical staff who are closer to management and may see matters differently from the wage earners. The British Transport Officers' Guild (BTOG) with a membership of only around 2,000, makes representations to the Board but is not a formal negotiating partner on management salaries. It has recently merged with another managerial union in an attempt to obtain some muscle but it is still far from possessing the power that, for instance, the British Airline Pilots' Association or the Merchant Navy & Airline Officers' Association can exert on occasions.

The ASLEF formerly represented something of an élite

among railway workers in the traffic grades; this is hardly the situation today, and past hostility between that union and the NUR has been a most unhappy feature. In the 1955 ASLEF strike those drivers and firemen who were members of the NUR (mainly in North East England and some on the London Midland Region) continued at work; and this increased a bitterness which has broken out at intervals ever since. Recently however joint action by the two unions has become much more likely as a *rapprochement* has taken place. Will it hold?

The general public has little sympathy with inter-union disputes, certainly not when they involve public hardship. Exasperation tends to rub off on railway managers as well, and the whole image of the railway suffers, as well as its financial position and prospects. One must note the recent preference for wars of attrition rather than pitched battles, fought by banning overtime and rest-day working, working to rule or sporadic interruptions to train services. These cause great public inconvenience but do not involve the railway staff in total loss of earnings nor the unions in depleting their funds through the necessity to provide strike pay.

One must ask whether the machinery of negotiation and the arrangements for joint consultation work as well as they are supposed to. The first obvious point is that the conciliation machinery was never, when it was devised, expected to deal with a regular annual series of wage claims such as continuing inflation has caused. The machinery was designed to cope with crises arising only occasionally; its numerous stages are not really adapted to the twelve-month periodicity of negotiation, which has often meant virtually non-stop work on both sides, since almost as soon as one claim has been settled, the next year's has been lodged. Clearly some longer-term arrangement, for instance linking general advances to the annual rate of inflation (indexation) would in theory seem attractive. But several powerful forces work against it. One is the Conservative Government's belief that inflation can only be brought down if wage settlements are, when possible, kept below the rise in the retail price index. The other is the theoretical 'ability to pay' of an industry that relies upon substantial Government funding. Should the same criteria as apply to private sectors industries be enforced in BR; in other words, should no improved business mean no increase in pay?

The unions have three objectives in lodging pay claims. The first is the basic one of protecting the wage packet against erosion through inflation. The second is achieving or maintaining comparability with other industries. The third is the continuing improvement in living standards to which most people in this country have become accustomed over the past 30 years or so. Here the issue becomes complicated, because these objectives *are* often achieved by railwaymen, through enhanced earnings from mileage bonuses, overtime and rest-day working, rather than through higher base rates. To this the unions object, on the ground that total staff numbers, and hence union dues, are thereby kept down artificially. Moreover, the example of those who voluntarily work longer hours is anathema to unions dedicated to the task of securing a shorter working week and thus spreading the work-load over more individuals.

No one can pretend that these differences are capable of easy resolution. Moreover they exist against a background of demands from the management side for greater productivity, something that politicians comfortably insulated from the industrial battlefield can insist that BR obtains before major new projects can be approved. The scope here is still, in principle, very substantial: universal acceptance of flexible rostering; abolition of locomotive secondmen (or drivers' assistants), except for training and route-learning purposes; abolition of guards on braked freight trains; one-person-operation (OPO) of all commuter services, are obvious possibilities. OPO it must be remembered can require staffed stations for ticket issuing and collection, whereas open stations with ticket checking left entirely to conductor-guards on the trains is the contrary system. Overlapping between the two systems may be difficult to avoid on some lines, so that the full theoretical savings cannot always be achieved. The Tyne & Wear Metro system though has managed the best of both worlds with one-person-operated trains and unstaffed stations, with ticket machines and automatic barriers at stations centrally supervised from an all purpose control centre. It is though a compact self-contained system and might be difficult to translate to some BR conditions.

How can the unions be persuaded that further reductions will not only, in the long term, probably ensure the continuance of something like the present rail network, but also the survival of the unions as a major force? One can suggest that their combination in a single Union of British Railways is the real answer. Such a proposal has in the past run into great difficulties, sometimes accentuated by a clash of personalities at General Secretary level. It may not be too cynical to suggest that the NUR should take a leaf out of big business's book and follow the accepted techniques of the successful merger. Not merely the prospects of the combined undertaking, but the position of individuals has to be considered. Those displaced by a merger must be placated by compensation and in some cases golden handshakes will be appropriate. Dignity can be often protected by transfer to a non-executive post such as Honorary President for life. These are quite practical and by no means unworthy expedients for achieving a worthwhile merger.

A minor, but helpful move would be the payment of all grades by cheque on a monthly instead of a weekly basis; this would slightly reduce the psychological gap between the TSSA and the blue-collar unions. The option of a weekly cheque now exists but is not very widely taken up. A system of temporary weekly advances to bridge the changeover period would be necessary, but the eventual savings from avoiding cash movements should, incidentally, be considerable.

It is perhaps not unrealistic to hope that negotiations with a single consolidated BR Union on an all-grades basis might lead to settlements looking further ahead than 12 months, taking into account the expected rate of inflation and also the expected BR financial results over the period of a Corporate Plan, for instance.

Joint consultation is another aspect of industrial relations in which various good intentions are expressed soon after nationalisation have not been properly fulfilled. The machinery is there, but one hears complaints from each side. The unions may say that so-called joint consultation too often amounts merely to announcing decisions already taken by management. The management side may complain that what starts as a joint consultation meeting is too often turned by the staff representatives into an attempt at negotiation on conditions which are excluded by the terms of reference. A further problem is that matters supposed to be confidential for the time being, perhaps on account of possible adverse public reaction, are too often leaked by the staff representatives to the media. Lastly, arrangements which have passed through the joint consultation machinery may still be rejected by staff and be the subject of local industrial action.

'Co-determination' or worker participation in management seems on the whole to work well in some other countries; it is in fact a legal requirement in Germany. Why then do we in Britain adhere so obstinately to the idea of battle lines drawn up on either side? The unions have more than once rejected the idea of formal co-determination through representation on the BRB, arguing that their representatives would be in a minority and consequently might have to acquiesce in decisions with which they did not agree, incurring odium from their union thereby and losing credibility.

But even so, one must ask why it is normal for a management proposal to be almost automatically rejected by the staff side when it is first mooted, even though it may later be agreed. The whole idea behind nationalisation was that the conflict of interests between the workers and profit-seeking managements would be resolved. One cannot honestly say that relations between the BRB and the unions today are better than those between the former railway companies and the unions. This is rather tragic. Yet, probably, no one is to blame. Men of the utmost integrity (it is invidious, perhaps, to mention names, but Sir Brian Robertson, for instance, had the universal respect of the unions) have striven to achieve an acceptable relationship; unfortunately the background factors of contracting activity and financial constraints have been too powerful.

The prospects are improved where a management-cum-staff takeover has been effected, as in the National Freight Consortium. But this form of Syndicalism in modern dress does not appeal to the unions. And the prospects of floating BR as a company in which staff would be offered participation at favourable rates seems remote. Yet Conrail in the USA, which was the subject of a Federal Government financial rescue operation, has done just that, and Conrail thereby has been able to get rid of some of the restrictive practices with which the railroad Brotherhoods were strangling the US railways. It has achieved notable improvements in productivity and turnover, so that its survival, long in doubt, now seems certain.

It is difficult to know how far the unions to which railwaymen so loyally adhere really respond to their members' individual aspirations. One may guess that the majority of railwaymen prefer, once their turn of duty is over, to go home and relax rather than spend time arguing in branch meetings. The official association of the rail unions with Socialist policy for transport has become largely meaningless since railway nationalisation, so long their chief declared objective, has taken place. With it the stimulus of a crusade or objective has gone and been replaced by some disillusionment. There is no great new policy that can form the subject of resolutions at annual conferences. And so the activists who feel that the railway unions have a part to play in achieving a fully socialised state have lost a major weapon in their armoury. It is illogical for socialists to oppose state boards (and state management at one remove) on principle, and there is a need for a complete rethinking of relationships. Yet unfortunately those who are prepared to spend time thinking and debating are too often only a vocal and untypical minority, not the sensible majority who are satisfied with proper living standards in return for a fair day's work, a property-owning democracy and by no means an oppressed proletariat.

Old traditions and old slogans die hard, and it may still be a long time before the unions can reappraise their role and come voluntarily into a more integrated relationship of management and staff. Perhaps it is really up to the Government to take the initiative; a Ministry of Railways might be the catalyst, or the essential third partner in a railway forum that might form a component of the National Forum for Industry that Sir Peter Parker advocated more than once.

13

Foes, Friends and the Environment

Britain has always had something of a love-hate relationship with its railways. Those who, not unreasonably, deplore the extent to which political influences today affect railway operation and efficiency, might remember that even under private ownership the railway companies were often the subject of either support or attack on (to some extent) political lines. The alignment of the political parties was not however consistent. In the earliest days, many Tory landowners opposed railway expansion, while Whig and Radical industrial magnates promoted it. Later, railways became part of· the national 'Establishment', offering (with a few notable exceptions) safe investment opportunities as well as settled employment. Criticism then came mainly from Liberal or Radical elements which complained about the exercise of monopoly power. Later came the call for nationalisation, first voiced by the Amalgamated Society of Railway Servants (the forerunner of the NUR) in 1894, and taken up by the Labour Party in 1900.

Just before nationalisation in 1948, and during the controversy over the Transport Bill, Labour spokesmen attacked the record of the railways, both inside and outside Parliament as a means of justifying the Party's nationalisation policy, while the Conservative Opposition sought to defend the companies. Ironically, once nationalisation had taken effect, the roles were reversed. Conservative politicians and the predominantly Conservative daily press began to criticise the Railway Executive, while the Labour Government defended its actions.

In 1985, however, while Conservative opinion and policies are distinctly cool towards the railways, Labour's support is not energetic. It is weakened by railway trade union disillusionment with nationalisation and their tendency to regard the BR Board as an employer, very much as if it were a private railway company.

Important changes in political attitudes to the railways have come, on the one side, from the contributions of road transport employers to Conservative Party funds, and on the other by the weakening in the influence of the railway unions within the TUC and the Labour Party, mainly due to their drop in membership numbers. Certainly the rail unions no longer exert anything like their former power, when railwaymen, coal miners and steelworkers, called the Triple Alliance, constituted the heavy artillery of the TUC. The net effect of these modern developments is to deprive BR of strong political support not only on both sides of the House of Commons, but also the Lords.

The extreme Conservative view (not quite, fortunately, the official Government one) was contained in a leading article in *The Daily Telegraph* on 26 May 1984. Headed 'Why pay BR more?'; it argued that

'due to attention being focused on the miners' strike, the grossly excessive settlement between BR and its manual workers has gone unnoticed. Some 7 per cent gross has been given to one of the worst industries for over-manning and restrictive practices, which has just been granted another overt annual subsidy of £1 billion (figleafed as public service obligation, for one of the greatest dis-services inflicted on the British people) with covert subsidies to boot. There is no quid pro quo, only the promise to "discuss productivity". This promise has been made year after year. Everyone knows that it will not be implemented . . .

'Though BR is not very good at running trains, it has proven adept at politicking and at getting money out of the Government. This enables it to ignore its customers, since if they take their custom elsewhere, as many now do since de-regulation, BR's subsidies rise to compensate for lost fares. It could face total absence of passengers with equanimity so long as the rail lobby in Parliament and outside ensured a continued flow of subsidies. . . .

'Disheartening light on the fossilisation of national life is thrown by the consideration that though rail now accounts for only 10 per cent of total freight and passenger mileage, its supporters dominate select committees, back-bench committees and other fora, and that by one means or another BR has managed to obtain a complacent media.'

Such a combination of mis-statements and prejudice is almost incredible. Particularly laughable is the suggestion that BR possesses a powerful rail lobby. The 'railway interest' at Westminster has long since melted away, though in the 19th century it was a formidable power in both the Upper and Lower Houses of Parliament. It seems almost unbelievable today that in 1865 157 railway directors sat in the House of Commons and 49 in the House of Lords even though only a proportion could be considered really effective as a united railway 'lobby'. The numbers fell steadily thereafter, but even just before the General Election of 1945, a few railway directors still sat in each House. Nationalisation killed off this potential railway lobby, with only a few Members sponsored by the railway trade unions left available to speak on railway matters. Today the railway managements are effectively silenced by the obligation not to step out of line with Government policy. BR is thus presented to Parliament almost exclusively by its sponsoring Minister for the time being, whose support may be, to say the least, lukewarm. He is not an advocate on behalf of the railways within the Cabinet, but rather assumes the role of a judge.

The media are more prone to criticise, to highlight shortcomings, than to dole out praise. A good example is the reporting of the Annual Reports of the Central Transport Consultative Committee, whose criticisms are headlined while any commendations are barely noted. No one who knows Fleet Street would find this surprising, but railwaymen sometimes need a thick skin!

The hostility (on principle) of a predominantly right-wing press to nationalised industries is difficult to counter but personal relationships with newspaper proprietors and editors can be more important than the efforts of professional public relations officers. Sir John Elliot has related how the Express group of newspapers was incessantly attacking the British Transport Commission until he arranged a luncheon between Lord Beaverbrook and Sir Brian Robertson. Sir Brian explained the BTC's policies at length, after which the group's editors were advised to 'cool it'. However, laying on special press trips in order to obtain good publicity for some new development – the Advanced Passenger Train, for instance – always seems to attract some of the gremlins that lurk in every large undertaking, with the result that next day the press will gleefully report that the train was late, or any other small mischance that befell.

A couple of quotations may illustrate some of the strange thinking about transport prevalent in some right-wing circles. The 1983 Serpell Report contained a pronouncement that 'there is no right to transport in the absence of payment for the resources consumed'. Now this is not a law of economics but a subjective, in fact some sort of moral, or ethical, judgment. And when looked at more closely, it is virtually meaningless. What is meant by 'payment' – payment in full, or a contribution towards the costs incurred? Every transport economist knows that matching prices to transport costs is a most elusive concept, only realisable within a wide range of averaging or cross-subsidisation between individual units of service. Even if it is taken to mean that total payments over a long period must be sufficient to cover total costs over that period, has Serpell forgotten that virtually every great city in the world providing urban transport, as the price of escaping traffic strangulation, expects only a contribution (which varies widely) from the fare box, towards the costs incurred. And what are the 'resources consumed'? Are they just the immediate financial costs, or the much wider costs to the community which only social cost-benefit analysis can uncover?

The second quotation comes from a pamphlet issued by the Centre for Policy Studies supported by the Conservative Party, and misleadingly entitled 'The Truth About Transport'. This reiterates the arguments originally developed by the Railway Conversion League for reconstructing railways as highways, and which have been exhaustively demolished, not least in the Coopers and Lybrand Report of 1983. The pamphlet starts with a comparison of the theoretical merits of road and rail as forms of transport, in which the merits of the road are compared only with the disadvantages of the rail. No mention is made of the precisely opposite factors, which could just as easily have been enumerated! But the quality of the writing can best be demonstrated by one quotation, a claim that 'the vast clumsy apparatus of railways' is maintained 'for a small and often privileged minority'. Of the almost 700 million rail passenger journeys a year, how many were made by this 'small and often privileged minority'? Do the commuters from Dartford to Charing Cross, the school children, students and old age pensioners using the railway fall into that category? Have all the well-heeled business executives (the real privileged minority, with their use of company cars) transferred *en masse* to BR? If indeed they would, then the estimated loss to the Exchequer of some £2,000 millions a year through the use of subsidised company cars would be sufficient to fund the railways handsomely for quite a long time!

In contending with this sort of crude hostile propaganda, and the more subtle lobbying carried on continuously by the range of business interests represented in the British Road Federation, the railways can only try to put the record straight by factual presentation, by reasoned argument and avoiding political pitfalls. Unfortunately the traditional allies of the railways – coal and the iron and steel industries – are all in decline rather than expanding, largely as a result of secular trends over which they have no control. So they are not beloved of Governments which acts as their bankers, nor of the trades unions who are fighting a rearguard action against declining membership and declining influence within the Trades Union Congress.

A few MPs from former railway towns like Swindon, Derby and Crewe do understand the problems created by low investment ceilings. Unfortunately the railway supply industry of the private sector, which used to constitute a major industrial interest – rail makers, locomotive, carriage and wagon builders, signal engineering firms, and so on, with large export businesses – is no longer a major pressure group with strong influence with the Department of Trade & Industry.

In the corridors of power, therefore, BR walks largely alone. Its nominally sponsoring Ministry is often more of a critic than a supporter, the press is frequently hostile, and there are no large power bases in industry allied to it. Its main outside lobby is the organisation known as 'Transport 2000', officially

Small-scale but useful restoration work: a good Victorian station (Greenwich, Southern Region) being cleaned up *(Author)*

The complex in which the APT was born – Derby Technical Centre *(British Rail)*

The former M & GN Railway's swing bridge over the River Nene; it helped to accelerate the closure *(Real Photographs, courtesy Ian Allan Ltd)*

BR's timetable contains a mass of useful information, but you have to read the small print! *(Author)*

supported by a mixture of the trades'unions and outside railway supporters, and with a certain amount of quiet unofficial support from within BR. Transport 2000's arguments are however often based upon its own ideas rather than official Board policy. Rightly enough, it stresses the environmental advantages of railways and the vast hidden costs of road transport; but its ideas for rail expansion and extension are sometimes questionable, partly because it lacks the financial and technical resources to undertake studies in depth. Against the huge membership and the funds available to the Society of Motor Manufacturers and Traders, or the Road Haulage Association, or the many trade associations linked for public relations purposes in the British Road Federation, Transport 2000 is a tiny David whose pebbles scarcely disturb Goliath.

BR's last allies are what may perhaps be called the irregular troops, the large army of rail buffs or enthusiasts. That their numbers are formidable is evidenced by the money spent on journals and books about railways, with several publishing houses specialising in this market. The total amount of money raised for the rail preservation movement is in total also very large indeed: some 137 bodies varying widely in size and financial stability are now members of the Association of Railway Preservation Societies.

In the past some professional railwaymen found the amateur enthusiast to be a nuisance – especially if he strayed into danger while seeking a good railway photograph. And during the Beeching and immediate post-Beeching period there was a feeling in some quarters in BR that the enthusiasts' lobby, with its nostalgia for steam (which BR was eliminating as fast as possible) was hindering rather than helping the public image of BR as hard-headed and profit-orientated. However, a more tolerant – indeed encouraging – attitude has appeared in recent years. Steam preservation societies have been allowed (on payment) to run trains over certain BR routes and a semi-commercial relationship has grown up with the private railways whose timetables are now included in the BR volume.

Of course, it may well be true that most of the volunteer workers on preserved railways arrive and depart by car (possibly because there is now no BR service since the preservationists are preserving what BR closed and disposed of), and that many of those who buy railway magazines seldom buy a railway ticket. But goodwill should never be thrown away, because it can promote a climate of opinion that, at many removes, can even help to influence the Governments. Many knowledgeable enthusiasts help to support BR in the local or even national press and also help in a small way to lobby MPs on railway matters.

The enemies of the railway sometimes try to link the activities of the enthusiasts with those of the professionals in order to suggest that railways are outmoded and that affection for them is pure nostalgia, that has nothing to do with the economics of transport. They sneer at grown men who seek to continue in adult life with the playing with trains that they enjoyed as boys.

This is a completely fallacious idea. It is a source of future commercial strength if the interest of the younger generation – whose spending power is going to grow – can be stimulated in any form of transport. Major airports provide viewing platforms for spectators, realising that this helps to increase air-mindedness in the young. BR does not yet generally provide special observation posts for train spotters though they are tolerated at most stations. And the interest of the enthusiasts is not exclusively antiquarian or nostalgic; today's young train spotters are just as diligent in observing diesel and electric traction as their fathers were involved with steam locomotives.

Throughout British history it has been a great source of strength to both the Royal and Merchant Navies that so many boys love the sea. No one sneers at week-end yachtsmen (not since Dunkirk, at any rate); and railways, like airlines, can cash in on this fund of interest and goodwill even if its assistance is indirect rather than immediately measurable in financial terms.

It is entertaining and instructive to compare the attitude to railways of the early 19th century 'conservationists' such as Ruskin and Wordsworth, with that of their counterparts today. From being villains of the piece ('Is there no nook of English ground Secure from rash assault?') by contrast with those voracious devourers of ground, the motorways and airports, British Rail today seems almost to wear a halo. Impact on the environment has of course both a negative and a positive aspect. The negative one consists in doing as little damage, and causing as little nuisance, as possible. The positive one rests upon adding features of interest and sometimes even of beauty to the landscape.

It must be said that the demise of steam, though regretted by many on nostalgic grounds, has greatly improved living conditions for householders beside the railway. It is not just that urban housewives have been able to hang out their washing with more confidence, or have their windows cleaned less often. The clouds of smoke that used to drift across many towns from large motive power depots could cause pollution and produce pea-soup fogs in winter.

And the noise of steam locomotives working hard, though music to the ears of rail buffs, (a highly nostalgic sound when, rarely, it is heard nowadays) formerly could be cursed for disturbing the sleep of dwellers in crowded cities. The throbbing of a diesel or the passage of an 'electric' is much less obtrusive, if less romantic.

Another change beneficial to the environment has been the virtual disappearance of the loose-coupled hand-braked wagon. Formerly those living within earshot of any of the marshalling yards of BR – of which there were no fewer than 973 at nationalisation, a figure scarcely credible today – were conditioned not merely to the puffing of the yard shunters, but the clash of wagon buffers. In the large hump yards (of which there were 94 in 1948) this might be a practically continuous noise, night and day. And it was also a sound heard, if only intermittently, at almost all stations that handled freight – 6,408 of them existed at nationalisation. How quiet, by comparison, is BR today!

And what about visual intrusion? Well, most lines of railway have, with the passage of time, become pleasantly absorbed into the landscape. Moreover, unlike our main roads, they are usually free from ribbon development, though admittedly the railway approaches to some towns and cities formerly attracted some industrial development of a pretty dreary character.

On the positive side, the railways, especially in the first half of their 150 years' existence, contributed a large number of noteworthy additions to the British landscape – graceful viaducts, interesting bridges, quaint tunnel mouths and, above all, a large number of stations with varying degrees of architectural quality. It is true that from the latter part of the 19th century until a couple of decades ago, the railway attitude towards its 19th century heritage was often rather Philistine. Buildings were originally designed by architects in a great variety of styles, ranging from the pure classical (Huddersfield) to the Italianate (London Bridge), Gothic Revival (St Pancras) or Elizabethan (Stamford). Too many were damaged by insensitive additions or clumsy alterations carried out by District Engineers with no architectural training. And there was for a time a tendency to condemn almost everything that was not recent with the pejorative adjective 'Victorian' and to prepare plans for replacing it with something which might be operationally more efficient but would probably have reflected the standards of a pretty poor period in English architecture.

Happily all that has changed, thanks to the enlightened outlook of several chairmen of BR and the enthusiasm of men such as Sir John Betjeman, David McKenna, Christian Barman, F. F. Curtis, and Bernard Kaukas, who have combined a deep feeling for what is best in the legacy from the past with, usually, a fully realistic knowledge of what is needed to run a railway today. It was a sign of the times when BR published a large and lavishly illustrated book *The Railway Heritage of Britain*, which contained entries on more than 500 historic railway structures, and with more than 750 illustrations. Such a book would have been pretty unlikely to appear, at any rate with official sponsorship, in the 1920s or 1930s, when plans (mostly never executed owing to shortage of investment resources) existed for demolition and replacement of a number of the buildings illustrated. In fact, some 600 BR buildings are now 'listed' and thus protected to a considerable extent under the Town & Country Planning Act, 1945. Others are protected by being sited in conservation areas.

The charm of the railways as they used to be is not just something enjoyed by eccentrics and rail buffs; it is something that a very wide, and increasing, public now appreciates. This is shown by the strength of the railway preservation movement and the number of people who work hard at promoting it, as well as those who willingly pay quite high fares to ride in steam trains. BR has happily changed from the stance it adopted in the 1960s, when it seemed anxious to flex its muscles and show just how modern, unsentimental and purely profit-orientated it was; it now recognises that there can be money as well as popularity in nostalgia, permits steam trains to operate for enthusiasts' excursions and even operates some itself at, usually, an adequate profit. It was an imaginative move to provide steam services over that most romantic of all scenic routes, the line from Fort William to Mallaig – an example now being followed in Germany by the Deutsche Bundesbahn.

But the really important question is the role that the railway can play in helping to protect the environment from now on. It is significant that the whole climate of opinion has altered over the past decade. From the late 1950s to the early 1970s, the environment was attacked from many quarters and some of the damage done is now seen to be probably irreparable. High-rise blocks which tickled the fancy of ambitious architects and over-enthusiastic local authorities are now seen to have been largely a blunder. Some are empty, many are vandalised, some are having to be demolished. Great areas of our inner cities were flattened by the bulldozer and many still await their intended alternative use. Vast slices of agricultural land were needed for motorway construction in ways that would have thrown Ruskin and Wordsworth into convulsions of rage! Farmers have grubbed up quantities of woodland and hedges to create huge prairies in East Anglia and elsewhere. Lastly, the useful and unobtrusive network of public transport has been pushed into a position of dependency, by the unrestricted growth of private transport irrespective of its true economic costs.

There are no easy solutions to these environmental issues. But sooner or later politicians, of whatever complexion, will have to take stock of the costs, some obvious and some still hidden, which a free-for-all in transport involves. It is clear that the unrestricted growth, since the abolition of the former 'A' and 'B' licence, of heavy goods vehicles both in numbers and in all-up weight has inflicted a totally unforeseen degree of damage on a road system, most of which was never designed, constructed or maintained to carry such traffic. Local authorities everywhere are being constrained by financial limits to carry out patchwork repairs, likely to last only a year or so and in effect a waste of money, in place of the thorough resurfacing that is needed. Bridge parapets are destroyed and bridges made unsafe through heavy lorry usage, and urban pavements over cellars collapse when 30 tons or more of lorry-weight are parked on them overnight.

Even the motorways which one would have thought purpose-built for such usage are giving way; the 1984 summer's estimate for merely patchwork repairs amounted to £107 million. It looks as though the overloaded M1 may need either almost complete reconstruction with the provision of an additional carriageway, or else duplication at staggering cost, before too long.

The explosion in car usage, though not guilty of equal damage to the highway system, has led to atmospheric pollution on a scale that we experience but ignore, while our descendants will be unable to ignore its consequence if the doctors' predictions are correct.

In the social cost equation one also must count the billions of hours spent behind the wheel by millions of citizens every year, many of which are not even productive of movement, when one reckons the proportion of time spent, especially in cities, stationary in traffic jams or awaiting green traffic lights. Of these billions of man (and woman) hours, only a small proportion today can be classed as voluntary or pleasure motoring; most are a direct subtraction from more important activities in either work or leisure. And, quite apart from the staggering cost of road accidents mentioned elsewhere, the incidence of coronary heart disease from the stress of motoring, especially car commuting, is substantial. 'Let the train take the strain' is probably the best advertising slogan that BR has ever produced, because it is the most justifiable. The road interests argue that the cure lies in the provision of more and better roads; restrictions upon any form of transport in favour of another, they claim, distorts the economy, and the expansion in road vehicle numbers reflects a popular demand which should attract an appropriate response from Government. All very well; but cigarette smoking, now considered to be dangerous to health, is also a popular demand and, like road transport, it yields substantial tax revenues to the Treasury. So the Government hedges; it does not ban smoking, but it does seek to discourage it by bringing the facts to public attention, and by gradual tax increases to induce people to think again about the free exercise of their democratic right to damage their lungs with cigarettes. A moral here for transport?

The fact is that we have in many areas an overloaded road system that apparently we cannot afford to keep in a state of repair to match the annual increase in road usage. Alongside it, we have 10,500 miles of railway, nearly all of which (if we exclude some of the Southern Region commuter network) is capable, with negligible outlay on improvements, of carrying greatly increased volumes of passengers and freight. In other words we already have duplicates to the motorway network – but with rails instead of tarmac surface, more productive, pollution free on electrified lines, vastly safer, and ready to carry more traffic.

14
Communication, Credibility, and Ways Ahead

Every large business, above all in the nationalised sector, needs not just to sell its product but also to communicate. British Rail has to communicate with the Government, with its customers and (largely through the media) with the general public to create a favourable image. So far as its sponsoring Department is concerned, in addition to personal contacts between the Chairman and the Minister or Permanent Secretary there are meetings between chief officers and senior civil servants, with paper after paper being produced, some private and confidential and others intended for a wider audience. A good example of the research that goes into these papers is contained in 'Productivity Performance', an analysis by the BRB of its productivity improvements over the five years 1977–82; others are BRB's 'Corporate Plan for 1983–88', and the Steering Committee Report on the potential for the conversion of some railway routes in London into roads. Politicians and local authorities have been given excellent short notes on railway problems and policies in the 'Rail Talk' handouts series. Such documents supplement the very readable Annual Reports, which persuasively present the railway case.

Contact with Governments can be tricky because of the uncertainty about what each new Minister's attitude to railways may be, and how much weight he (or she) may carry with Cabinet colleagues and the Prime Minister. It is unfortunately true that politics is the art of the short-term, while railways respond to change only in the longer term.

Politicians are always looking for some gimmick which will gloss over the real problems of the railways and promise a quick financial improvement. It may be integration, or competition, or decentralisation, or rationalisation, or re-shaping, or privatisation. BR responds to these demands with varying degrees of enthusiasm or resignation – much depending upon the character of the chairman for the time being – and produces document after document as Ministry-fodder.

A senior civil servant in the Ministry of Transport was once asked by the author to say what his first reaction was when he received a submission or report from BR. He replied 'I immediately look for anything that could possibly embarrass the Minister'. Nothing about, for example, the likelihood of improving public service, or greater cost-efficiency! He was of course discharging the main duty of the civil service, the protection of Ministers, however ineffective, from criticism, however justified.

Politics is not merely the art of the possible; it is the art of over-simplification. To present a busy politician with all aspects of the sort of complex problem that arises in railway work is virtually impossible. Dangerous short-cuts have to be accepted. They are dangerous because when things take an unexpected turn there are recriminations; and the defence, that the issue had had to be oversimplified, is not usually acceptable.

A good deal can of course be done by building up personal contacts, by luncheon meetings with politicians and senior civil servants at which briefing and 'off the record' exchanges can take place. A delicate question is how far an Opposition 'shadow' Minister should be briefed, especially towards the end of a Government's life so that, if after the election he comes into office overnight, he can be reasonably well informed. A chairman of BR may have to judge how far such contacts are legitimate without embarrassing the existing Minister. There are certain unwritten civil service conventions on this subject which help to keep the machinery of Government oiled despite changes of gear.

BR has also a need to communicate with staff and the joint consultation machinery was devised for that purpose. In addition, 'open forum' meetings were held in the Southern Region at intervals in the early years after nationalisation, where regional managers appeared on a platform to answer questions posed by staff of all grades on any subject connected with their work. Useful within limits, these occasions were not easy for management since (unlike Ministers answering questions in Parliament) they had no forewarning of the issues to be raised and no opportunity to brief themselves about what could be matters of detail in their departments.

In spite of the joint consultation procedures, management often has to accept that in practice there exist two channels of communication with the staff; one is via the managerial organisation and the other, in parallel, via the union organisation. Unless information reaches staff at local level through both chains simultaneously, difficulties can arise. Either management is accused of by-passing agreed procedures by being over-hasty, or it is considered slow and ineffective in comparison with the union network.

BR tries hard to sell itself to the staff via *Rail News*, a tabloid which mixes information with 'pep' articles, critical correspondence (and replies), and gossip about personalities. Of its kind, it is bright and readable.

But the best kind of communication, from the human aspect, is one that is difficult to practice in very large organisations but is nevertheless important. After Lord Ashfield retired from the London Passenger Transport Board chairmanship and became a Member of the British Transport Commission, his successor at LT invited the Commission to visit the LT works at Acton. Touring the works in a party soon bored Lord Ashfield, who knew the story better than the guide. He moved away on his own and as he walked down the line of machines, every now and then he stopped, greeted a workman by name and discussed with him personal health and family matters, in which Lord Ashfield's memory of individuals was fantastic. Call it paternalism if you like; it was a marvellous morale-booster.

The problems of communicating adequately with passengers are huge. Considerable efforts have been made in recent years to improve matters and yet there is still a long way to go. It has always been accepted that the timetable is a selling document of prime importance. The free pocket timetables issued for individual services are excellent in principle. The main problem is their all too frequent non-availability in the racks at travel centres. This usually may be a result of local management failing to re-order in time, though printing delays can cause an intractable situation.

The disappearance of the big poster time-sheets from stations is in some ways to be regretted, though admittedly the alphabetical lists of main stations for which departure times are shown offer quick reference. But they do not show intermediate stops, nor the provenance (and intermediate stops) of trains arriving at the station, both points on which people meeting trains may require. Is there not usually space for both alphabetical station-lists and timesheets to be displayed at almost all stations?

The summary timetable booklets are of only limited value to people who travel a good deal, who need to ascertain connections for through journeys and so on. For them – as for most offices, hotels, clubs, and public libraries – the complete BR timetable is essential, since the demise of Bradshaw, though its price, at over £3, is something of a deterrent to the individual traveller. But the computer-produced complete BR passenger timetable has been issued in a type-size so small that only those of good eyesight, in a strong light, can easily decipher the contents.

The concentration of passenger train telephone enquiries on a limited number of designated area offices is a sound idea in principle. Its main drawback is the extra cost that an enquirer may have to meet, as compared with making a local call to a local station. It is justified, because of the uncertainty surrounding calls to stations where the telephone may be in the booking office, and the booking clerk, if he is busy, may of necessity either ignore the ringing or answer it curtly and possibly unhelpfully. The centralised enquiry offices, however, are rather too often the subject of public complaints about inability to get through – a sign that the number of exchange lines on the switchboard and the number of staff employed are inadequate. Admittedly, to provide resources able to cope promptly with peak hour enquiries may mean that they are under-employed at other times, but if the system is to be made to work, that price may have to be paid. Pre-recorded tapes have their uses, but they cannot answer every question that the enquirer may wish to put.

As for station announcements, inevitably they will be

compared with airports; airports are not most people's favourite places, but at least there one can usually hear clearly the messages coming from the public address system, often in several languages, rather different to the unintelligible booming noises that too often resound in BR stations. Of course, high glass roofs create a resonance that can be difficult to cope with, and throbbing diesel engines do not help either. But there are some obvious points. First, the pitch of a female voice is usually much more clearly audible and intelligible than the gruffer tones of most men; this is noticeable at those stations where a lady announcer alternates with a male colleague. (One may except some pre-recorded announcements made for the Southern Region by a clergyman with a suitably parsonical intonation!)

But surely the answer at large stations lies in using loudspeakers of low power to reduce the booming, but in much larger numbers and much closer to ear level. Powerful speakers 15ft above the ground are liable to create a Babel in the upper atmosphere, at any station.

A small matter which has received insufficient attention is the elimination of railway technical terms or jargon from the announcers' vocabulary. The public finds it odd that trains are delayed owing to a 'track failure'. (They envisage the rails lying in a heap somewhere.) The correct term is surely 'an electrical fault'. Apologies for trains lacking their usual number of vehicles should not be due to 'shortage of stock' but 'shortage of carriages'. 'Reaction' is another operating term that can mystify, and a 'broken rail' suggests an alarming gap in the metals, rather than a crack or a flaw, as is usually the case.

The rapidly growing provision of public address equipment on trains poses problems. Some guards use it with zest, others play it down. Some 'hope you will have a pleasant journey', and remind passengers to collect all their belongings if leaving the train. Others are silent on this point. One or two exuberant souls have been known to sing or whistle to cheer up their passengers. This is far removed from the 'correctness' of the German or Swiss railwayman. The British usually refuse to submerge their individuality, but this sturdy characteristic has to be reconciled with proper communication, which is after all a major requisite in a service industry. Problems can also arise with strong ethnic accents, though some can be attractive, as an agreeable West Country or Welsh voice in an IC125 leaving Paddington!

So far as communication with the general public and potential rail users is concerned, the obvious medium is television advertising. BR has concentrated upon discount fares (very wisely) with a certain amount of gentle 'knocking' of the opposition, namely road transport. It is perhaps arguable that the 'knocking' could, in line with today's advertising practices, bring out the true costs of car ownership, the environmental and social costs of road haulage, and the productivity improvements on the railways. Railway publicity has been fighting with the gloves on; perhaps it is time to get down to bare knuckles.

The desire to project a prestigious image nowadays seems to involve establishing a 'corporate identity'. BR is in good company here. Many years ago Frank Pick evolved the Underground's bulls-eye station sign which 75 years later is still London Transport's hallmark. Almost as significant was the sans-serif typeface designed by Edward Johnston for Pick and used ever since for all Underground and London Transport display work. Close behind came the LNER with its own typeface, 'Gill Sans' designed by the sculptor Eric Gill, and the lozenge-shaped logo. Since those days the scope of corporate identity has embraced rolling stock liveries and many other details, with so much importance attached to it that one might imagine that a railway needs a logo before it needs a locomotive.

BR got off to a hesitant start after nationalisation, with the BTC's deplorable 'bicycling lion' wished upon it, and its own design of inter-twined sausages – a sort of elongated London Transport bulls-eye – for station names and other signs. The modern corporate identity emerged in the mid-1960s; it covered locomotive and carriage liveries, typography and signs at stations and elsewhere, with the universal use of the double-arrow logo. It was enshrined in Corporate Identity Manuals, strict observance of which was required by headquarters.

The corporate identity programme certainly achieved standardisation. New station signs – for the first time using lower-case letters – in black and white replacing the former

189

regional colours are universal, or nearly so. (The undefeated GWR spirit has allowed a number of large, typical 'Great Western' station signs to remain alongside the 'corporate identity' ones on the Western Region. Long may they stay there; they are fine, legible and full of character – more so than the modern, sans-serif lower-case lettering alongside.)

But a certain dissatisfaction with the rather dull, if serviceable, blue and grey 'corporate identity' rolling stock livery, now 20 years old, has grown up. The first break-away came with the livery chosen for the Advanced Passenger Train with pale grey below the waist and above the windows, dark grey around the window area, and bold red lining; this style of contrasting colours has since been adopted for the HST IC125 units on which 'Executive' service is offered. Other styles of livery have been developed for specialised or dedicated services, for example the orange and grey of trains for Strathclyde PTE. Unfortunately the benefit from the adoption of more attractive liveries is thrown away unless really strong managerial control can be exerted to ensure first that similarly painted stock is kept marshalled together and, second, that it is properly cleaned. In fact, a brightly painted train in dirty condition can look worse than a drab one in a similar state, for the contrast between paint and grime is all the more obvious. Subject to that, there is much to be said for more adventurous colours and styling.

Apart from the channels and the techniques of communication, one must ask how effective is the message received. There may be a credibility gap between the aspects of BR seen from top management level from the heights of Rail House at Euston, and actual performance as viewed by the customer, uninterested in policy and long-term planning and concerned only with the detail of service quality. An excellent concept can have its effect seriously damaged by small shortcomings with which top management finds it difficult to concern itself, as for example small nonsenses in the timetable ('arrives 2min later on Saturdays'), failure to top up lavatory tanks before a journey starts, rough riding in commuter trains, or scruffiness in a buffet car.

Sir Peter Parker's famous phrase about 'the crumbling edge of quality' can be taken literally, because it is at the edges, not at the centre, where crumbling occurs. Sir Peter was referring to the inadequacy of investment ceilings to allow for even essential renewals, but crumbling is noticed by the public in countless tiny items not necessarily dependent upon investment finance. Many of course are the public's own fault; it is not railwaymen who foul train toilets, vandalise stations and carriages and steal compartment lamp bulbs. But the war against these minor anti-social elements must go on for the sake of the well-behaved majority; if it appears to be going badly, then it is BR's credibility that suffers.

There are both long-term and short-term answers to the crumbling edge. In the long term, more investment is needed; without it, the system will wither away slowly. But it is no good waiting for long-term benefits without energetically making the best of what is available in the meantime. The London & North Eastern Railway had fewer investment resources than the other three main line companies, but within this constraint it was aware of the need to achieve quality control. One example of this was the post of 'East Coast Inspector', whose staff were constantly travelling on the railway's prestige services and noting minor shortcomings or causes of complaint by passengers. Another was a system of station improvement committees, composed of representatives of all the main departments, touring the system and (although not empowered to spend any substantial sums of money) attending closely to the 'crumbling edge'. One recalls a very bulky file in the chief general manager's office entitled 'Good Housekeeping at Stations', a subject in which that officer took a close personal interest.

The pressures upon a BR chief executive today are probably such that he could not be expected to follow this example. But there could be a case for a quality inspectorate independent of the regional organisations, constantly touring the system and noting where action needs to be taken to prevent or rectify a crumbling edge. Otherwise how can the centre be informed correctly about what happens at the perimeter apart from, say, the Annual Reports of the Central Transport Consultative Committee, which do not always make very comforting reading?

A quality inspectorate should have a dual responsibility to the centre through the Sector Directors, on whose payroll it should be, and to the regional managements with which close liaison should be maintained. Hopefully, any initial objections on the part of the latter could be removed if the inspectorate's reports are submitted jointly to the Region and the Sector, with responsibility for action left to the former, though of course follow-up reports would ultimately be made to the Sector.

Would this lead to cross-purposes, to friction, or the creation of superfluous new posts? On the contrary, it should enable better use to be made of today's equipment by eliminating small nonsenses and failures of a kind that are liable to appear in any large organisation that does not exercise close quality control. In organisation theory, delegation (such as BR has to practice very extensively) needs to be associated with control, in the sense of monitoring performance, with a flow of information upwards matching the transmission of authority downwards. BR has perhaps not been as strong in the former function as it has in the latter. Strengthening its communications in the field of quality control should increase its credibility with the ordinary passengers.

This book has been a purely personal view of BR in the mid 1980s; it ends with a personal 'shopping list' of factors that may determine whether the ways ahead for BR tend to lead upwards or downwards. They are grouped under two headings: external factors over which the BR Board has little or no control, and internal factors made within the Board's control.

External: The Attitude of Governments

The Conservative Government which took office in 1979 and returned in 1983 has been dominated by economic and political philosophies that are not helpful to BR in general. On the other hand, Government measures to ensure more effective democracy in the trade union movement could be advantageous, helping to stabilise industrial relations in the long term.

How far would a Labour Government – or a Social Democratic/Liberal Alliance Government – support the railway, as an environmentally beneficial form of transport, more effectively? Much could depend upon whether the railways can get across to Ministers, civil servants and the public, the reality of the 'social contract' which exists between the State's railways and the State's citizens.

Monetarists and 'supply side' economists bristle at the mere idea of a social contract, because they draw a sharp distinction, often superficial and misleading, between what is social and what is economic in transport. They like to believe that transport is akin to manufacturing industry, dominated by simple inter-action between supply and demand, whereas it is only partially an industry. It is also a public service that is an essential requirement of any advanced society, and it is in addition a personal activity, e.g. motoring, carried on largely regardless of economic factors.

The idea of a 'social contract' between major transport systems and transport users is not a moral or philosophical one; it is based on the very nature of the demand for transport and the nature of transport costs. Cross-subsidisation is inherent in all public transport, if only because matching supply to demand in point of time is usually impossible, there being no such thing as storage or warehousing of transport services. This means that the relationship between cost and price is immensely variable – peak and off-peak services within the 24 hours being the most obvious example. Then there are the joint costs arising from the need to operate out-and-home. Hauliers subsidise 'return load' quotations from profits on the outward trip; feeder railway routes are subsidised by earnings on the main lines . . . and so on.

The social contract exists partly because a railway has to provide a service which cannot *in detail* be charged for on a basis of unit cost. Hardly anyone will want a season ticket to London, if the last train homewards leaves at 6.30pm because the railway management finds that trains are too lightly loaded to be economic after that hour. Transport needs to offer a comprehensive service, taking the rough with the smooth, unlike the 'cowboy' operators who jump in and out, picking out the profitable routes or times of the day and ignoring the others. This is something that coach operators, for instance, for the moment can do, while the railway has to commit its resources to a comprehensive day-long service.

Is a transport free-for-all, with the State restricting support for its own network while independent operators cream the traffic, really a policy at all? In the end, the demand for comprehensive transport services must outweigh short-term benefits from sporadic competition. One would not deny that there may be a temporarily invigorating effect from de-regulation and more competition; but in the end there must come a shake-out and the organisation that accepts a social contract must outlast the fringe operators. That was the experience in London's passenger transport in the 1920s – a cycle of private semi-monopoly, then free-for-all competition, then combination, and lastly regulated public enterprise, which may well have to be repeated in the 1990s because we cannot afford to let private transport destroy public transport while being unable to replace it.

Perhaps a future Government will come to office with a real transport policy. If so, it will be the first since 1945, and even then the policy had not been thought out adequately. Maybe the concept of public expenditure upon improving the nation's infrastructure – transport, sewerage, water supply, fuel and power – will not then be dismissed as equivalent to digging holes and filling them up again, which appears to be the view of some monetarists.

Meanwhile, it would be helpful to get away from the idea – first sold to the Ministry by consultants who did not spend long enough in the railway world to grasp the realities under which it operates – that there are completely self-contained businesses within the activity of running trains which can be given separate and realistic financial targets, to be met by specific dates. So far as central Government funding of BR is concerned, it has been suggested in Chapter 8 that global support, replacing the Public Service Obligation, should be given for all the Sectors, subject to an 'efficiency audit' to establish that BR is meeting the requirements of the public as effectively as possible. There is a good precedent for this in the annual reviews that were made by the Railway Rates Tribunal in the inter-war years to justify the continuance of the charging scales sanctioned by the Tribunal.

Of course, payments from PTEs and local authorities in respect of area support for local services would be additional to and outside this central review, as there is a contractual relationship here and BR's corporate customers other than the central government can satisfy themselves directly that they are getting value for money.

External: trade union attitudes

It would be a hopeful sign for the railway industry if the move towards more union democracy – ie participation by rank-and-file union members, preferably by secret ballot, in all important decisions – became a fact and not just an ideal. Is action always to be inaugurated by an often militant minority? The traditional loyalty of railwaymen and their sense of comradeship makes them prone to respond to a call for industrial action whenever an activist or group of activists calls for it, whether or not the original cause is fully understood. There is another major point. Some union leaders do not seem to realise that unofficial action is an attack upon their leadership as much as upon that of the management. Too many of them are inclined to accept it as helping in the running struggle with management, rather like a general who welcomes guerilla activity supporting the regular troops. But if unions are to be seen as responsible, and able to negotiate agreements that will be honoured on their side, they should crack down very heavily, with suspensions or other disciplinary measures, upon unofficial industrial action by their members that really undermines their authority. Officially disowning such action while privately condoning it weakens the standing of the leadership with both their own members and with management. Perhaps a new generation of union leaders will take this point.

External: the fuel cost equation

Future economic historians may conclude that Britain in the 1980s was living in a fool's paradise, with a disastrous balance of payments with the outside world temporarily masked by the exploitation of North Sea oil. BR's policy statements on electrification have stressed the desirability on national grounds of reducing the consumption of oil – whether imported, or from North Sea sources – in terms of our future situation as North Sea supplies decline. Even the chairman of Shell has told his shareholders that 'coal is by far the closest alternative to oil and natural gas and the probably major beneficiary from switching away from oil. ... The great advantage of coal is that it is much more abundant than oil.

Present recoverable coal reserves would probably last for 255 years at present rates of consumption'.

But these facts have not yet penetrated sufficiently to induce the Government to approve a really long-term railway electrification programme. Its reaction to rising world prices for oil has been essentially a short-term one; first, to keep up domestic prices (through taxation) in line with those in non-oil-producing countries; next, to push up electricity prices so as to reduce the incentive to change from oil; and lastly, to force up the price of gas to follow the rise in electricity. The whole position was temporarily distorted by the secondary effects of the 1984–85 coal strike.

But short-term expedients cannot in the long term completely conceal the underlying situation. Coal and nuclear power stations are the only final answer to Britain's industrial power needs, and a steadily growing rail traction demand would help to put the balance right. When at last this will be recognised may depend upon events in the major oil-producing areas, as much as upon re-appraisal of the remaining reserves of North Sea oil and gas, or new thinking at Government level.

Internal: re-deployment of management talent

It should not be too easily assumed that the total number of managerial and administrative staff on BR today is necessarily excessive, as some critics have suggested, in relation to the total workload. The abolition of Divisions and the move to a two-tier managerial structure within the Regions has reduced numbers by shortening the chain of responsibility from top to bottom. But that of itself will not necessarily reduce the basic work-load; it only eliminates some 'post-office' work at Division level in the transmitting of orders down, and information upwards. It is an elementary organisational principle, that if you shorten the chain, you widen the span of authority. The need substantially to strengthen the powers of area managements after the abolition of Divisions was therefore obvious.

But, arguably, a further shift is required. Too high a proportion of management talent has been devoted to planning and higher administration – and arguing endlessly about the railway of tomorrow – not enough to ensuring that the railway of today is run as efficiently as possible with its existing resources, both physical and manpower. This is partly a consequence of Government pulling up the plant by the roots every few years to examine its health, leading to many of the best brains being taken out of the business of running trains, or fixing fares, and directed to fashioning mathematical models with computer techniques for a possible 21st century system. Yet BR is judged by its paymaster, the public, much more upon present-day levels of performance than upon forecasts of future improvement, however impressively presented.

It may be appropriate to redirect into quite basic tasks within the Regions some of the talent that has been sucked away into the stratosphere of headquarters planning. A better public image of BR probably depends upon more top management effort concentrating upon details such as cleanliness of rolling stock, information systems for passengers, train punctuality, station appearance and amenities, and (very important) train catering; effectively this means rather less concern with long-term policy objectives, however worthy, and more with today's performance quality.

One would like to see more senior management in evidence on a 24-hour basis, with higher-powered officers in charge on Saturdays and Sundays, on a rota system. Too often there seems to be a shortage of supervisors and managers of senior status after 6 pm on Friday until 9 am on Monday. Yet it is over the weekends and at night that things seem most often to go wrong. At a lower level, one would like to see more travelling ticket inspectors working at weekends and on late evening trains, because that is when out-of-class travel and, more of a problem, vandalism and hooliganism, are most likely.

Redirecting more management talent into keeping the railway running on a day-to-day basis should be accompanied by an upgrading of some key posts that have not been sufficiently highly rated in past years including area managers, controllers, station supervisors, heads of timing and diagramming sections and those responsible for rostering drivers' and guards' duties. For instance, everyone who plans the timetable is exercising a function vital the railway's economic and operational efficiency. Yet too many weaknesses creep into today's timetables, despite – or perhaps because of – their production by computer – and higher-graded staff may be needed to deal with even detailed planning here.

Finally, in management talent comes 'Control'. Quick decisions, based upon exhaustive knowledge of the system, are needed to cope with and rectify any operating problem. Anyone who uses the railway regularly with some knowledge of the background will have encountered cases when 'Control' does something quite inexplicable even to the staff on the ground. Inexperience or too-junior status can lead to wrong or delayed decision. Shift controllers and supervisors or regulators in centralised power signalboxes have a heavy responsibility, and their calibre, training and remuneration could well be reviewed. The total cost of upgrading such posts would in total be insignificant in relation to potential gains in efficiency.

Internal: Definition of the Inter-City Sector

The concept of Sector Directors seems to involve a contractual relationship with the Regional General Managers whose objectives and duties must be to run the railway and provide services to standards laid down, and of course discussed and agreed to be feasible, by the Sector Directors. The latter have the tasks of planning ahead, and thereby they enable the Regional General Managers to concentrate upon day-to-day management; but they must also engage in close service quality monitoring and should have their own staffs for this purpose.

If there exists such a customer-and-supplier relationship between the Sectors and Regions, it was never at all logical to combine the post of Sector Director (London & South East) with that of General Manager, Southern Region, because one individual is then responsible to himself, not a good organisational practice! It is in no way derogatory to the talented first holder of the joint post to suggest that its ending in 1985 was a sensible reform.

There is a case for taking all the Southern's longer-distance services away from the commuter-dominated London & South-East Sector (just as some Eastern Region services from Liverpool Street and the Victoria-Gatwick Airport trains have been transferred) and in consequence making the Southern's General Manager responsible for achieving standards of service on these trains acceptable to the Sector Director (Inter-City). If this were done, the Sector Director (London & South East) would be free to concentrate upon the huge task of overseeing the London daily commuter movement in terms of service quality – timetabling, design of rolling stock, regional performance, especially in speed and punctuality, fares policy, London Regional Transport liaison, and so on.

Admittedly many of the Southern's longer-distance trains are also used by daily commuters. But this need not be an obstacle to introducing or maintaining Inter-City standards on them. (The Western Region does just that between Reading and London.) The following services seem to fall naturally in the purview of the Sector Director (Inter-City):

> Waterloo–Bournemouth/Weymouth
> Waterloo–Exeter
> Waterloo–Portsmouth
> Victoria and London Bridge–Brighton
> Victoria and London Bridge–Bognor/Littlehampton
> Victoria and London Bridge–Eastbourne/Hastings
> Charing Cross and Cannon Street–Hastings
> Charing Cross and Cannon Street–Folkestone/Dover
> Victoria–Ramsgate/Margate/Dover

Introducing Inter-City service quality on these routes is now due.

Internal: Investment priorities

Within limited overall investment ceilings, should priority be given to projects that will mainly reduce costs, or to projects designed directly to stimulate traffic? In the first category one might place most re-signalling schemes; in the second, new rolling stock and station improvements. Of course there is some interaction between the two classes of investment but even so, a critic could argue that cost-reduction has dominated revenue-stimulation too much in the recent past.

If this is true, responsibility lies to some extent with Government. Both politicians and civil servants live in the world of budgets and expenditure control, rather than that of enterprise and profits. The way to keep down BR's financing requirement that appeals to them is reducing expenditure rather than stimulating receipts. The spiral effect of cutting down, in worsening service and thereby reducing receipts still

199

further, is something that is shrugged off, because it does not happen immediately, whereas the savings will appear in next year's accounts. It is also usually easier to sound convincing about potential savings than to prove a future increment in revenue. And inside BR there are powerful technical interests with pet schemes employing the most modern technology, offering departmental prospects of interesting occupation for several years, that have little or nothing to do with immediate benefits to the rail user.

The other question is the merit of a single large, spectacular, project, a main line electrification for example, which absorbs resources that, diffused throughout the system, would have produced, for instance, better passenger carriages and many stations cleaned and facelifted if not reconstructed. The answer, if the best is not once again to become the enemy of the good, is to insist that electrification must be financed 'below the line' – that is, excluded from the annual ceilings on investment which do little more than cover major renewals and maintenance. The probable difficulty is that the Government insists upon lumping the annual outlays upon an electrification scheme together with all the other items in the investment budget, thus presenting BR with a dilemma of priorities. During the early years of the execution of the 1955 Modernisation Plan, expenditure upon items contained in the plan was kept separate from the 'normal' investment requirements of the railways. This precedent should be applied to a long-term electrification programme, if a Government can be found courageous enough to approve one.

Internal: BR Needs a new 'Square Deal'

One cannot criticise BR for any failure to present the railway case in well-argued reports and pamphlets. But these have not been aimed at the general public so much as at the (presumably) informed minority. The presentation, mainly on TV, of the general railway image has relied until recently too much on the rather unconvincing 'This is the Age of the Train'. That has now been replaced by 'We're Getting There'. But something more in the nature of a crusade is needed, to drive home the facts of the railway situation and to try to enlist public support, with a change into top gear and a louder and clearer message.

A prototype exists in the 'Square Deal' campaign of 1938/39. This was aimed at persuading the then Government to change its traditional attitude to railway charges – that they must be regulated to protect the public as though railways were still a monopoly. To this end leaflets, pamphlets, press advertisements and posters were lavishly employed to present the railways' case. And it was successful, in as much as in the summer of 1939 the Government agreed to give effect to the railways' application. Only the outbreak of war prevented that taking place.

The object should be a railway that in AD2000 will match or better any in Europe – or Japan. But a crusade would need to be supported by intensive management effort to bring up service quality everywhere to the standard of today's best on BR, or even better. Such a visible overall improvement could spring from a major reduction in those small failures and weaknesses which create a disproportionate amount of public criticism. Attention to all the details of performance as has been suggested above would give maximum credibility to the proposed crusade.

To conclude: perhaps the best guarantee of a bright future for BR, and an emergence from any twilight uncertainty about future Government support, lies in following the classic definition of genius as an infinite capacity for taking pains. All the problems of size, or remoteness of top management from the standards of performance at local level, can certainly be overcome by utilising the talent that already exists within the management structure, and much better than by engaging expensive consultants looking for a problem to suit their solution!

Appendix

The Railways Then and Now in Figures

People often like to compare BR of today with 'the good old days' of steam traction. Some have vivid personal memories; others rely on what they have read or seen in pictures, and the recollections of older folk. How far back should one go in seeking comparisons? Probably two reference points for comparison with the 1980s can be picked out: the year 1938, because it was the last 'normal' year before the second world war and before Government control was instituted; and 1947, the last year before nationalisation.

Does one seek to evaluate changes in quality, or in quantity of service? Some figures about train services have been given in Chapters 1 and 5, but they cannot measure such factors as punctuality, reliability, cleanliness, and so on.

Seeking quantitative comparisons between BR in 1983 (the latest year for which statistics are available as this book goes to press) and the railways of 36 years ago and 45 years ago respectively, bristles with difficulties. The statistical sources comprise the BR Board's Annual Report for 1983, the British Transport Commission's Annual Report for 1948 (which includes 1947 figures), and the Ministry of Transport 'Railway Returns' for 1938. There is considerable variation between these documents, both in regard to the quantity of information and the method of presentation. To begin with, the railways included in the 'Railway Returns' are not exactly those nationalised in 1948 to form British Railways. Then, the vast changes in organisation between 1948 and 1983 – above all, the 'hiving-off' or privatisation of sections of the business – create difficulties. The BRB's Annual Reports now only publish a fraction of the statistical information provided in both 1938 and 1947. Lastly, changes in methods of traction are an obvious factor affecting the presentation of comparative figures; and metrication (tonnes for tons) is a minor complication.

Subject to these reservations, however, the following tables highlight a number of dramatic changes, the reasons for which have mostly been discussed in this book.

British Railways Statistics

Assets (at end of year)	*1938*	*1947*	*1983*
Route-miles open for traffic	20,007	19,639	10,541
Track-miles open for traffic	52,357	52,254	25,664
Stations open (passenger & parcels)	n/a	1,886	2,366
Stations open (freight only)	n/a	1,593	253
Stations open (passenger & freight)	n/a	4,815	nil
Station refreshment rooms	n/a	431	223
Marshalling yards	n/a	973	50
Steam locomotives	19,646	20,023	nil[a]
Diesel locomotives	43[b]	55[b]	2,603
Electric locomotives	13	16	247
Loco-hauled passenger carriages	43,492	36,073	4,059
Non-passenger carrying carriages	18,321	15,313	2,156
Diesel multiple-unit vehicles	126[c]	40[c]	2,703
Electric multiple-unit vehicles	2,133	4,232	7,306
High Speed Train vehicles	nil	nil	709
Advanced Passenger Train vehicles	nil	nil	30
Wagons	663,589	1,223,634[d]	54,510

Notes

(a) Standard gauge; there are three 1ft 11½in gauge locomotives for the Vale of Rheidol line

(b) Includes petrol locomotives

(c) Mostly 'railcars'

(d) Includes ex-private owners wagons acquired by Transport Act, 1947

Appendix

Work Load	1938	1947	1983
Passenger journeys (*millions*)	1,236	996	695
Passenger miles (*millions*)	n/a	21,259[a]	18,700
Average length of journey (*miles*)	17.27	24.3[a]	27.0
Freight originating tonnes (*millions*)	289[b]	272[b]	145
Net tonne-miles (*millions*)	16,672[b]	21,457[b]	10,653
Loaded train miles (*millions*)	421	338	230
Average length of haul (*miles*)	59	75	73
Average wagon load (*tonnes*)	7.2[b]	7.8[b]	29.0
Loaded wagon miles (*millions*)	3,003	3,252	411

Notes
(a) 1948: estimated
(b) Tons

Index

205